ADHD

REFLECTIONS ON
A HIDDEN DISABILITY

By

Angel Crouch

Copyright © Angel Crouch 2015
This book is sold subject to the condition that it shall not, by way of trade or otherwise, be lent, resold, hired out, or otherwise circulated without the publisher's prior consent in any form of binding or cover other than that in which it is published and without a similar condition including this condition being imposed on the subsequent publisher.
The moral right of Angel Crouch has been asserted.
ISBN-13: 978-1515393313
ISBN-10: 1515393313

This book is dedicated to my children – Jordan, Lewis, and Taylor, and to all the children and young people with a difference I have had the privilege of working with.

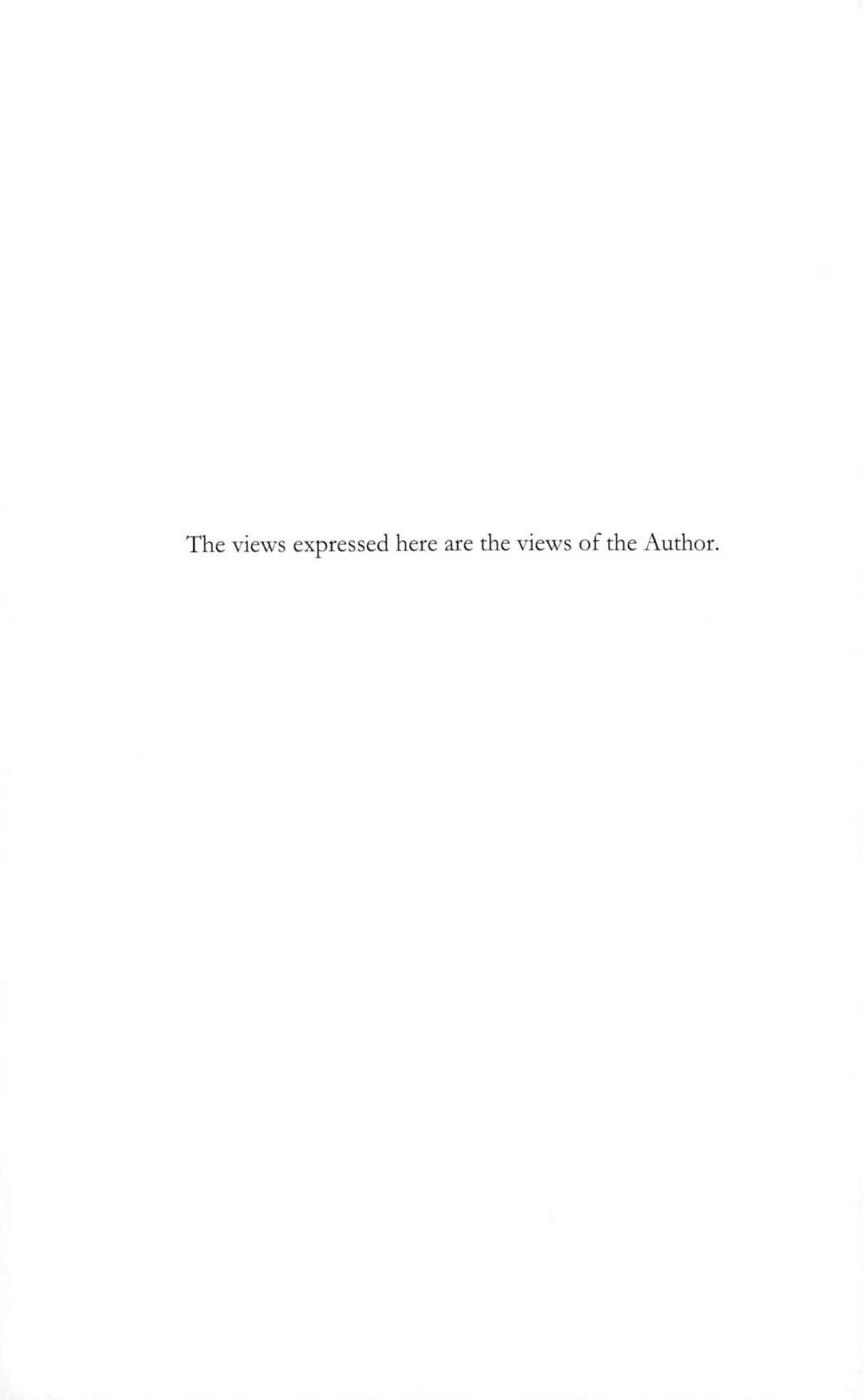

The views expressed here are the views of the Author.

CONTENTS

Foreword i
Preface iii
Chapter 1. *A Square Peg in a Round Hole* 1
Chapter 2. *A Definition of Sorts* 4
Chapter 3. *Parent Experiences* 25
Chapter 4. *Child Experiences* 31
Chapter 5. *The Different Approach* 39
Chapter 6. *Commonalities and Consideration* 41
Chapter 7. *ADHD Voices* 47
Chapter 8. *Top Tips* 57
Chapter 9. *Self-reflection* 74
Chapter 10. *Some FAQs* 80
Chapter 11. *Conclusion* 86

Foreword

I have worked many years with Angel, supporting families by helping them manage and understand their ADHD child. I have been so impressed how he has a natural empathy with them and can build up a trusting relationship when other professionals have failed.

Many parents have told me they have been waiting a long time for a comprehensive book that is not judgmental and will have more insight into the condition, and most importantly learn some practical strategies so they can get back the confidence that has been lost in managing their child's condition. For too long parents have felt it is somehow their fault and I hope this book will dispel some common myths.

I never knew Angel's personal journey until I read the book and how it has informed his approach to his work. I hope you will find it as helpful as I have done.

Jean Waitt
(Social Worker)

Preface

Over the course of my journey through life I've been privileged to meet some remarkable individuals with one thing in common: Difference.

Difference can be hard to understand; difficult to tolerate; irritating to experience; frustrating to support and, challenging to appreciate. ADHD is an example of such a Difference.

My four and a half years as Specialist ADHD Parenting Practitioner for a North London Council supported learning, participation and encouraged social inclusion of all children and young people with ADHD. The role delivered evidenced-based parenting programmes and provided advice, information, and training on strategies to support better educational and social opportunities for children with ADHD, tackling underachievement and overcoming barriers to learning.

The role helped children have better educational experiences, improved life choices and chances, and enhanced social and community involvement. This early intervention and preventative nature of my role relieved the burden on Social Services and strengthened multi-agency support for vulnerable families, thus increasing their life choices and opportunities.

My motivation was to change the way people view ADHD. I wanted people to explore different ways of responding or dealing with the challenges ADHD gave rise to. I wanted to halt the damage I saw being done to children with ADHD by the ill-advised need to control and cure them. I wanted to assist children with ADHD to improve the quality of their relationships with others by developing their self-esteem and confidence in their ability to learn. The positive feedback I received from children with ADHD, their parents, and professionals confirmed that such change is possible and can be achieved.

Behaviour problems are the most commonly reported reasons for children's difficulties with social relationships and learning. Young people with Attention Deficit Hyperactive Disorder (ADHD) need a lot of support in dealing with the academic challenges and the social hurdles presented by the condition.

ADHD-related behaviour problems can cause distress to the child, family, and community, and can lead to high levels of public expenditure. Academic and social development may be adversely affected, leading to further long-term life problems, which may include drug and alcohol dependency, mental health difficulties, relationship breakdowns, and poor work histories. Also, having the unfortunate label of a mental illness means they are also more than likely to be perceived as aggressive, dangerous to others and themselves, and having a potential for violence.

My own childhood was different to the norm, yet it was normal because of the difference. During my early formative years in England, I was raised by a foster family. The early separation from my birth family gave me insecure attachment and trust issues. Relocation to West Africa with my birth parents at age eight gave me separation, loss and resettlement issues. Boarding school from age nine until sixteen gave me social anxiety and relationship issues. Some traumatic childhood incidents gave me sleep difficulties.

My point is that due to a mixture of disaffected childhood and negative life experiences, it is difficult to determine where one issue starts and another ends. Nevertheless, what I consider to be the key issues of ADHD have always been present in my life. I am restless, fidgety, hypersensitive, and moody. I experience social confusion, black and white thinking, body dysmorphia, forgetfulness and social anxiety. I have an addictive personality, and I suffer from depression, a lack of empathy, a rigid sense of justice and power and control issues. I indulge in self-talk, and make noises (especially when anxious or frustrated). I even have the infuriating habit of interrupting others and completing their sentences. I have spatial awareness and distance perception problems and this list is not exhaustive!

All these aspects of my character have had an impact personally and professionally on how I view the world, but I do manage my life with the coping skills that I have developed along the way. I hope to demonstrate in this book how you can support and help your child manage the many and varied features of ADHD. By sharing some of my reflections on the individual differences that I have experienced, I hope to empower parents and enlighten the understanding of others.

There are already numerous books, loads of self-acclaimed experts, and an assortment of training programs that lay claim to being able to treat or in some cases cure ADHD, a condition on which much has been written, yet very little translates this understanding into effective support for those who have it. So I hear you ask: 'What is different about this book?'

This book does not promote a cure as there is no cure for ADHD. It will however, hopefully empower you and enable you to have a greater understanding of the condition and give you some ideas of how to manage it in a less stressful manner. It will also give you an appreciation of the daily struggles that people with ADHD face in their lives.

I believe that the best way to learn about a condition like ADHD is from the people who have been diagnosed with it. This book captures a snapshot of the experiences of such individuals.

Chapter 1

A Square Peg in a Round Hole

ADHD is a developmental condition, so it follows that there is no immediate antidote. As children develop, they learn coping strategies to enable them to get along better and fit in with others.

A person with ADHD is a square peg that society tries to fit into its round hole. Teachers and parents inadvertently act as agents of society, challenging the free will of these square peg children with ADHD. The more you try and shave off the differences of that square peg and force it into the round hole, the more damage you are doing to it. In essence, you are further disabling a child who already has a disability.

If a child has impaired eyesight, teachers and parents make reasonable adjustments and would therefore not expect that child to read from the whiteboard like everyone else.

If a child had one leg, the PE coach would make reasonable adjustments and not expect that child to jump over a hurdle like everyone else.

Yet if a child has ADHD, parents and teachers still expect them to sit still, not interrupt, wait their turn, not swear, remember what they learnt last week, not procrastinate... I hope you get the picture?

This makes for an unhappy child. To make the square peg fit into that round hole, adults create a set of unrealistic expectations, and start chipping off bits of that square peg, consequently damaging it.

Children with ADHD are the ones who best know how the condition affects them but they may not always be able to express this in an appropriate or meaningful way. Often, their comments are dismissed because firstly, they are a child and therefore don't really know what they are talking about. Secondly, the manner in which their comments are expressed: shouted, cussed, and sworn – will often make the recipient of the communication switch off, and so important messages are lost.

Here are some examples of real ADHD Voices, a snapshot of comments from the children and adults with ADHD. I hope it helps enlighten you about some of their frustrations, their anger and their coping strategies which are all individual experiences of ADHD.

Some of the children with ADHD that I have worked with said:

> I get angry cos no matter how hard I try, it's never good enough.

> Grown-ups are always telling me to shut up.

> No one wants to be friends with me.

> I keep getting told off!

> I don't mean to keep interrupting but I can't help it

> My head feels like a Tumble Dryer.
>
> People only notice the bad things I do.
>
> When people wind me up, I get told: Ignore them. **It's not that easy!**
>
> I always seem to be in trouble.
>
> I hate it when people shout at me.
>
> I always forget what I'm supposed to remember but I can't help it.

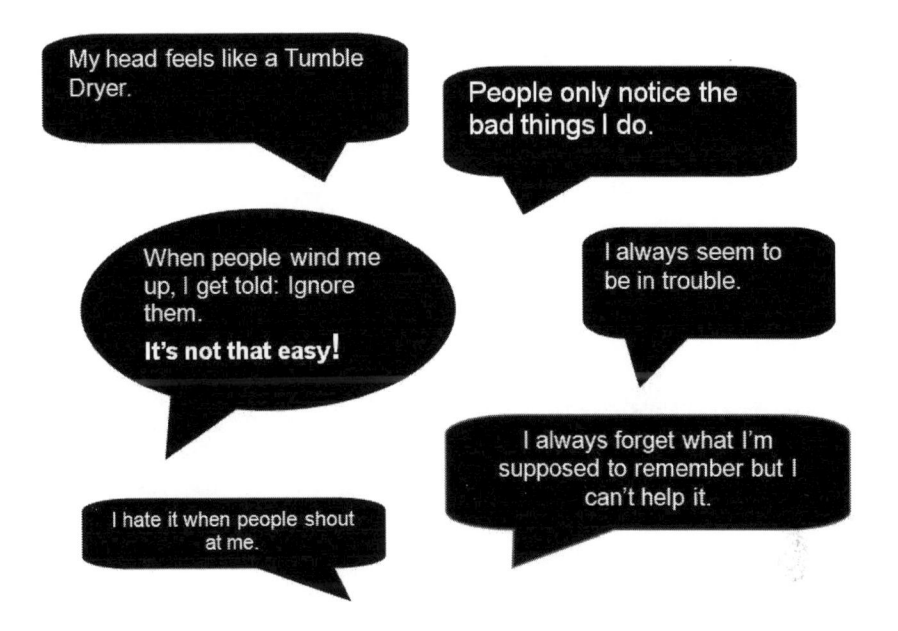

It is not surprising to hear children with ADHD express such frustrations, as having a brain difference means they are programmed to behave differently. They are expected to behave typically but they have difficulty in doing so. Consequently, their presentations are habitually challenged, usually in the form of negative, forceful and controlling communications. So is it unsurprising that they start to feel bad about themselves or begin to feel resentment towards others, and believe that the world doesn't understand them?

Hopefully while reading this book you may think:

"That sounds just like my child…"

"I always wondered why he did that."

"Now I have some idea of what she means when she says 'I can't explain it.'"

I really hope you will understand how what other people say and do affects the children who have been diagnosed with the condition.

No two children with ADHD are the same and no child with ADHD has ADHD in isolation. I hasten to say that this is my personal experience, but my claim is based on over twenty years of practical experience of working with children who have such a difference.

Chapter 2

A Definition of Sorts

Attention Deficit Hyperactive Disorder (ADHD) is a real condition and not a made up one, despite what certain people think; but the definition does, in my opinion, need updating.

ADHD is not only about hyperactivity, inattention and impulsivity; ADHD affects the way information is processed, stored and retrieved. ADHD is responsible for deficits in working memory, speed of processing, reasoning, emotional regulation, time and distance perception, organisation, and sequencing. ADHD affects mood and conduct. The brain is overwhelmed with too much information much too quickly, which is then processed too inaccurately in a brain that has diminished ability to suppress internal and external sensory input. Consequently the body and mind do not cooperate with the individual and the result is atypical presentations over which they have little control. ADHD, despite being invisible, makes those who have it think, feel, and behave differently.

In trying to add more detail to the standard information guides about ADHD (i.e. subjects are inattentive, impulsive, hyperactive), I am mindful that often, children with ADHD have parents with ADHD; parents who will have had similar childhood experiences to their own children. They may experience the same difficulties with reading, writing, understanding, perceiving, hearing, smelling, processing… the list is endless. I have therefore tried to explain my experiences of ADHD in a practical manner.

The medical definition of ADHD describes the symptoms of inattention and hyperactivity but impulsivity, a trigger for both mood and conduct, is just as significant yet is not mentioned in the acronym.

My definition of ADHD is more practical and would describe the feelings and the moods that impel the behaviours:

A is for Anxiety

D is for Discontent

H is for Hyperactivity

D is for Depression

These are the issues that I feel impact most on the presentations of children and adults with ADHD but I do believe that there is a need for an ADHD spectrum that describes the extensive range of conditions that can co-exist with ADHD. The following graphics are my contribution to that spectrum

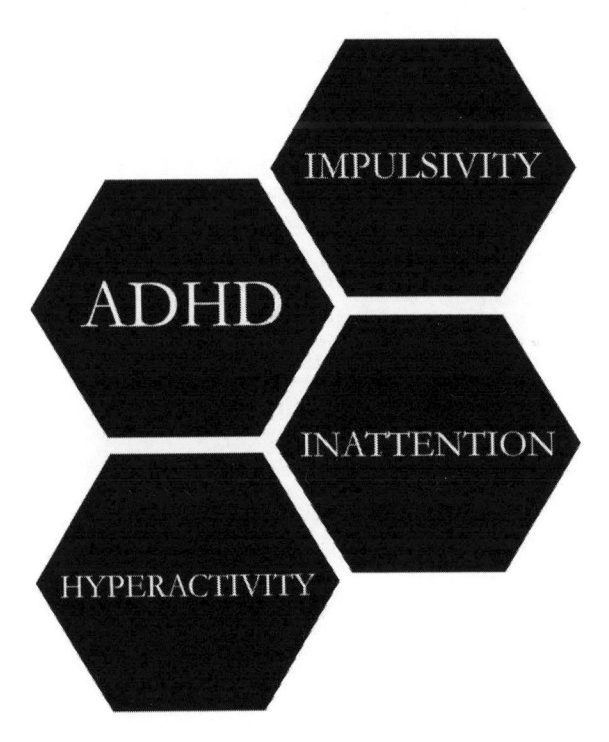

ADHD

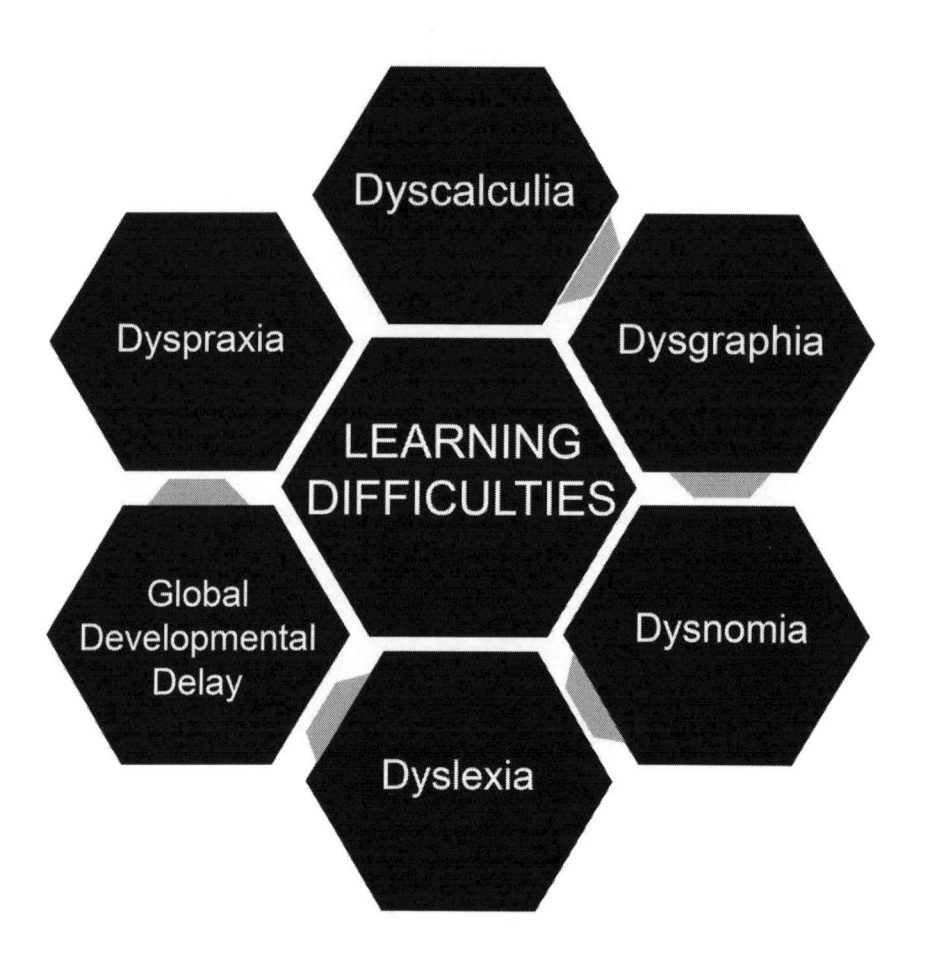

Learning Difficulties

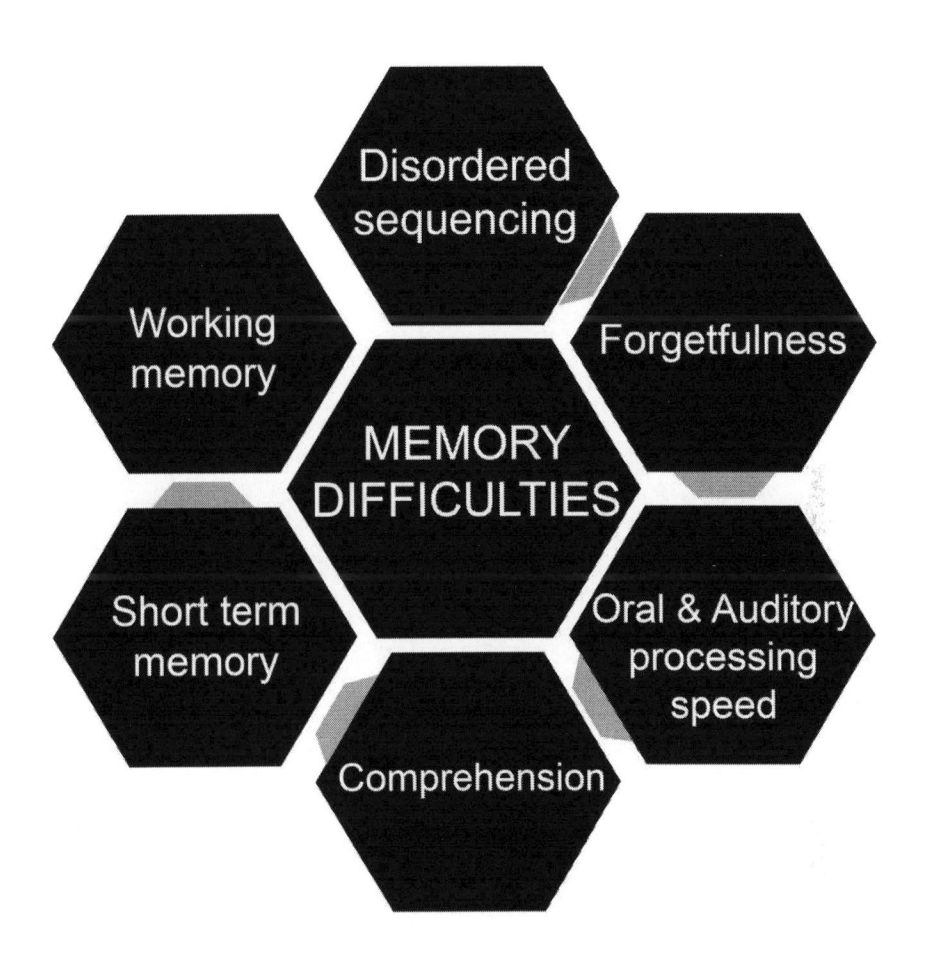

Memory

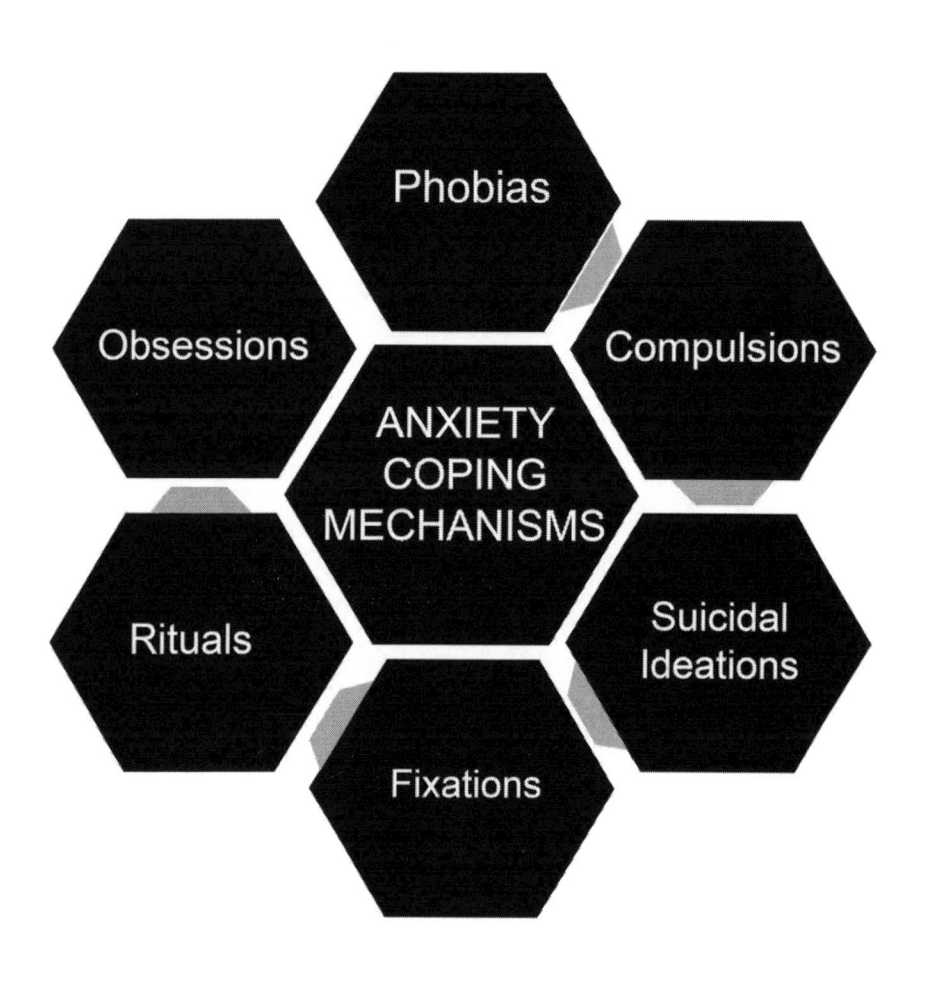

Anxiety

PERCEPTION & AWARENESS

- Heightened or Reduced Body Awareness
- Poor Eye Contact
- Compulsions
- Distance Perception Difficulties
- Fine & Gross Motor Skills Problems
- Low Self-esteem Negative self-perception

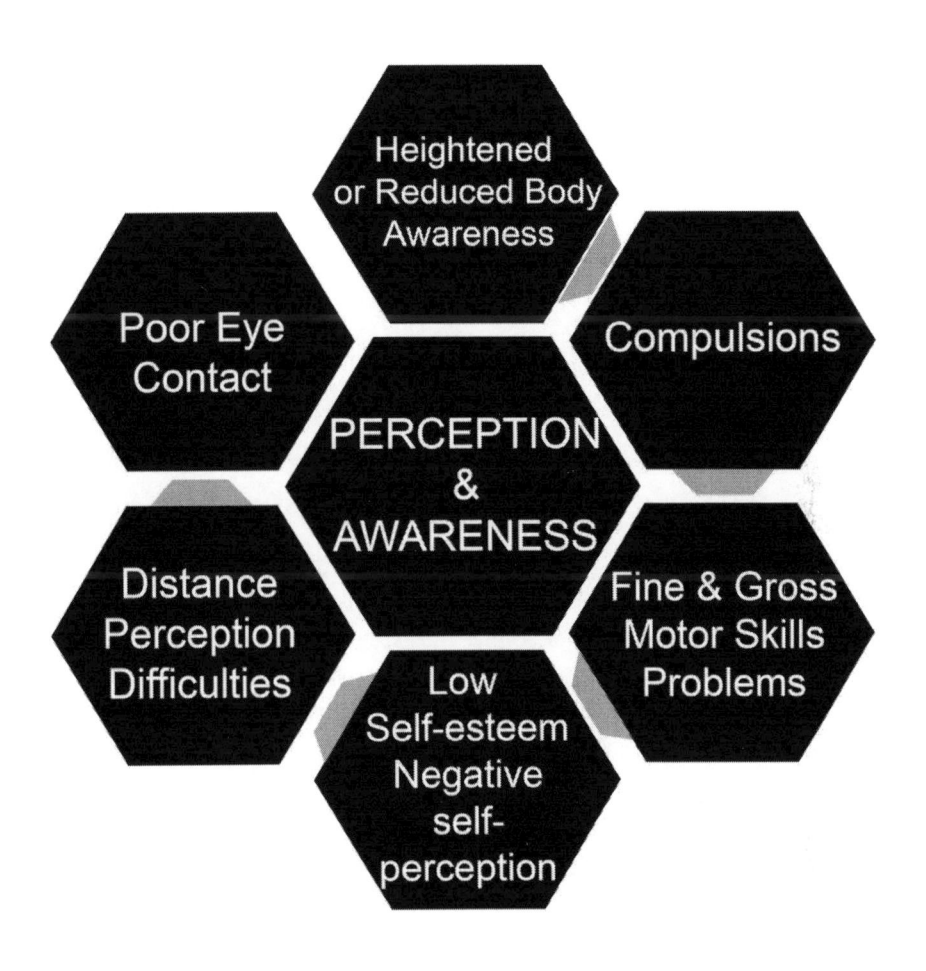

Sensitivity

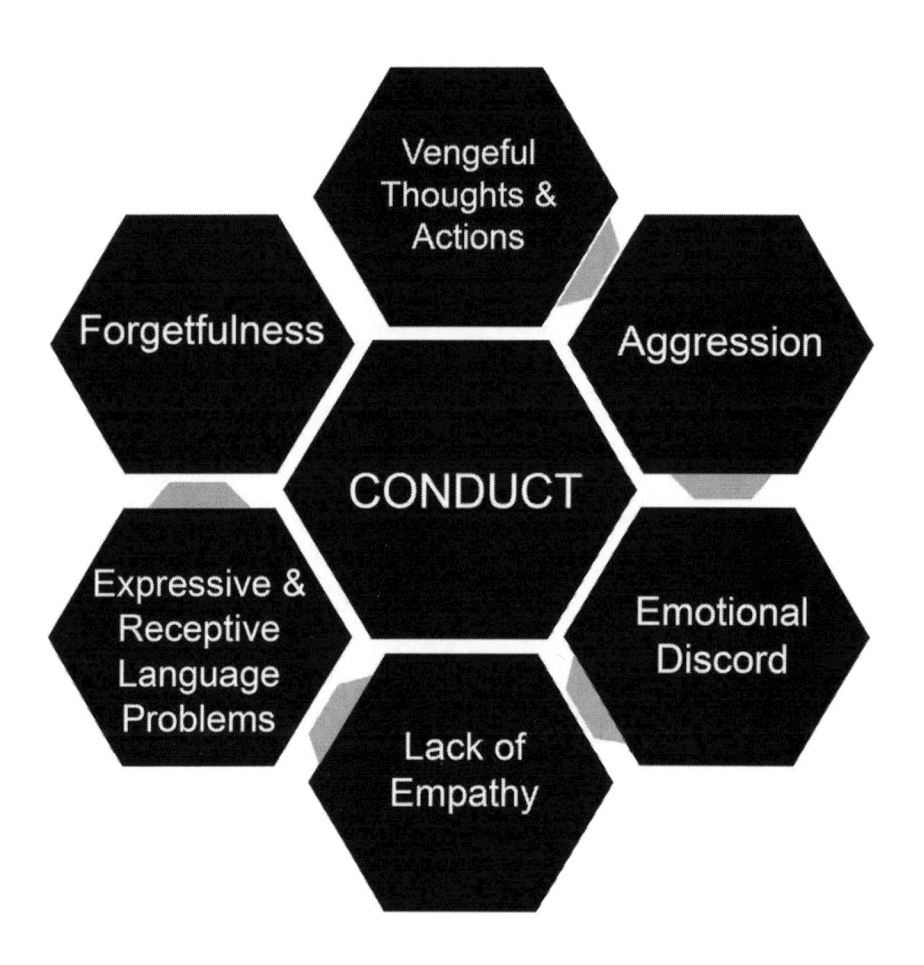

Conduct

MOOD AFFECTS

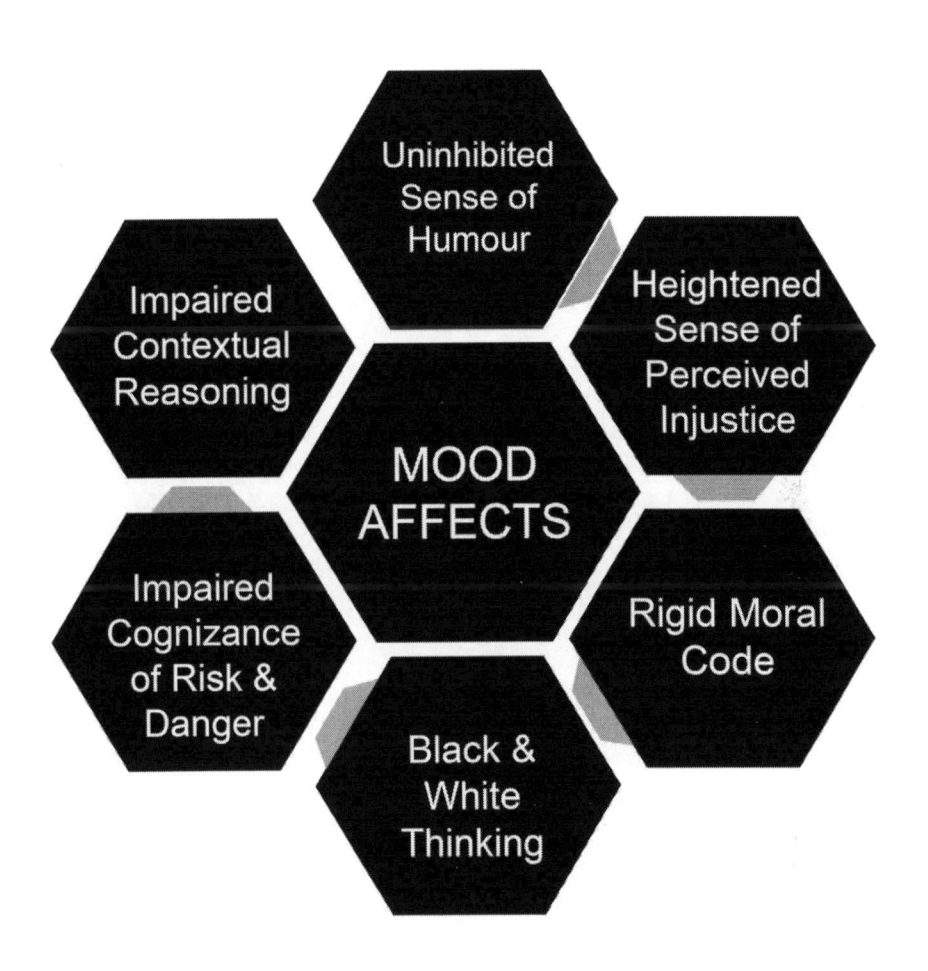

- Uninhibited Sense of Humour
- Heightened Sense of Perceived Injustice
- Rigid Moral Code
- Black & White Thinking
- Impaired Cognizance of Risk & Danger
- Impaired Contextual Reasoning

Mood

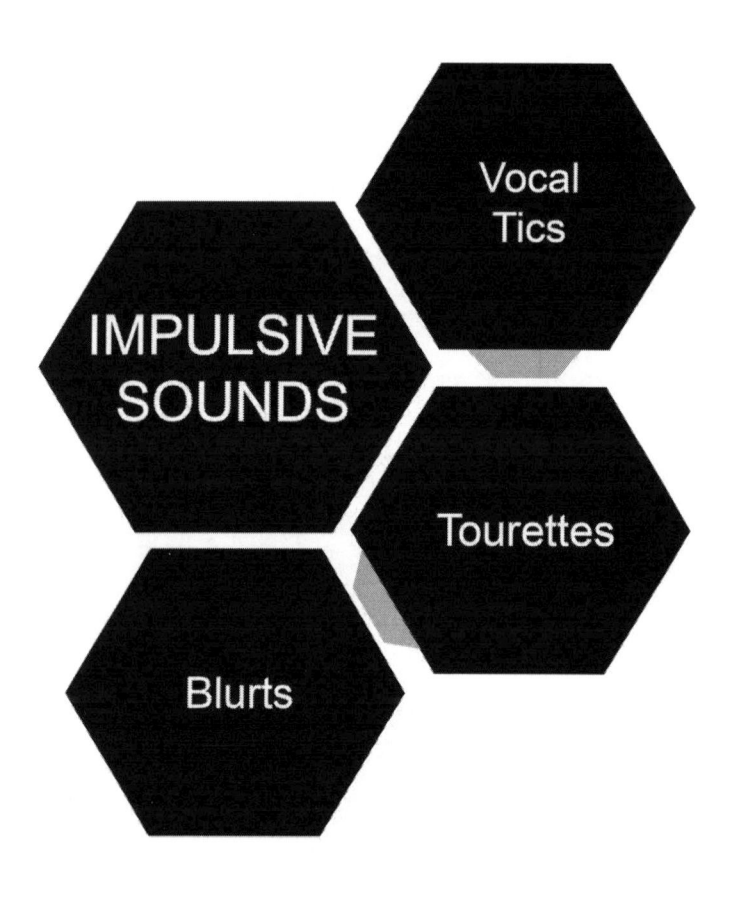

Noises

Some Other Co-Morbid Presentations

I haven't yet met an individual with ADHD who presents as having just difficulties with inattention and hyperactivity. Even if this were the case, the acronym ADHD does not take into consideration the many other hidden issues such as memory impairments and sensory deficits. My opinion is that the current definition of ADHD does not adequately capture nor explain the variety of difficulties that subjects experience. My vast experience of children with ADHD is that there is usually some other additional emotional or neurological problem. Some children are lucky (or unlucky) enough to have a definition of more than just ADHD, but most are not.

In some cases, these additional problems are "secondary" to ADHD — that is to say, they are activated by the frustrations of coping with symptoms of ADHD. For example, a child's prolonged lack of motivation and underachievement may cause them to experience anxiety in school. Or, years of disapproval and negative feedback from parents, teachers and peers may cause a child to become depressed. In some cases these secondary problems may resolve on their own, once the child's ADHD symptoms are supported to become less intrusive. In a lot of cases however, the secondary problems are distinctive "comorbid" conditions caused by the same elements that trigger the ADHD, and thus will not just disappear despite improvements in coping with ADHD. These problems will require additional or different treatment.

The range of co-morbidities of ADHD is varied and can be dependent to some degree on the resilience of the individual with ADHD and the levels of negativity they face in their environment. For instance, one child may react to habitual social exclusion with anger (external) while another child subjected to the same negative influences may respond by withdrawing and may experience depression (internal) negativity.

Children with ADHD will inevitably experience some level of learning difficulty, so let's take a closer visual look at some of these learning difficulties which by their very nature are disabling to the normal development of children who have them. Note the additional practical problems that can apply. Hopefully, this will provide an improved understanding of just how complex ADHD can be.

Towards a Spectrum of Learning & Communication Difficulties

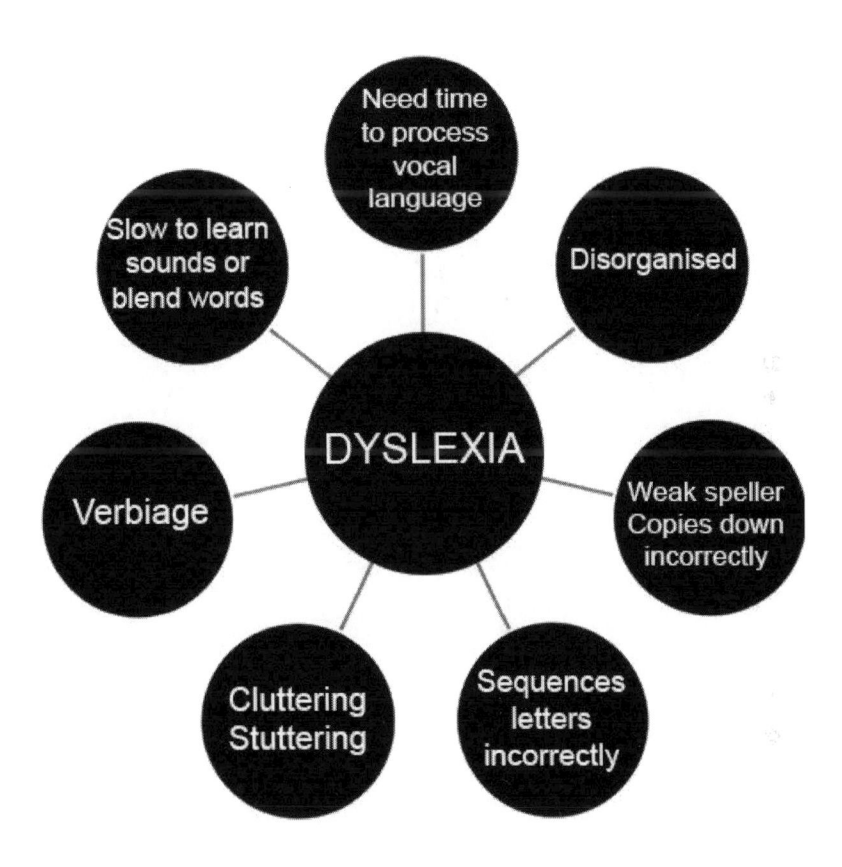

DYSLEXIA
- Need time to process vocal language
- Disorganised
- Weak speller / Copies down incorrectly
- Sequences letters incorrectly
- Cluttering / Stuttering
- Verbiage
- Slow to learn sounds or blend words

Reading & Writing Difficulties

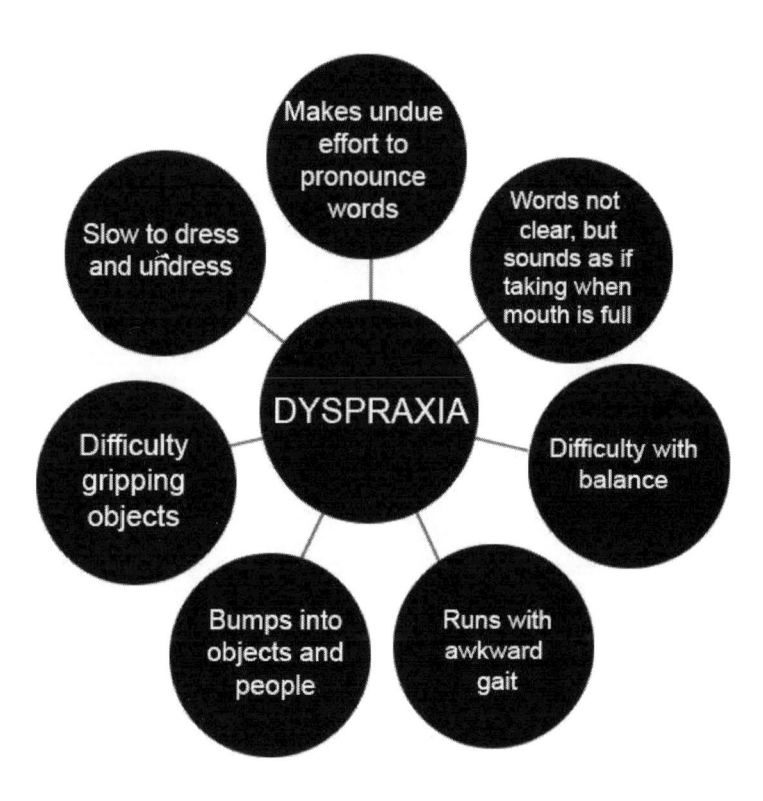

```
                    Makes undue
                    effort to
                    pronounce
                      words
                                      Words not
      Slow to dress                  clear, but
      and undress                   sounds as if
                                    taking when
                                    mouth is full

      Difficulty        DYSPRAXIA      Difficulty with
      gripping                            balance
      objects

         Bumps into         Runs with
         objects and        awkward
          people              gait
```

Physical expression & Coordination

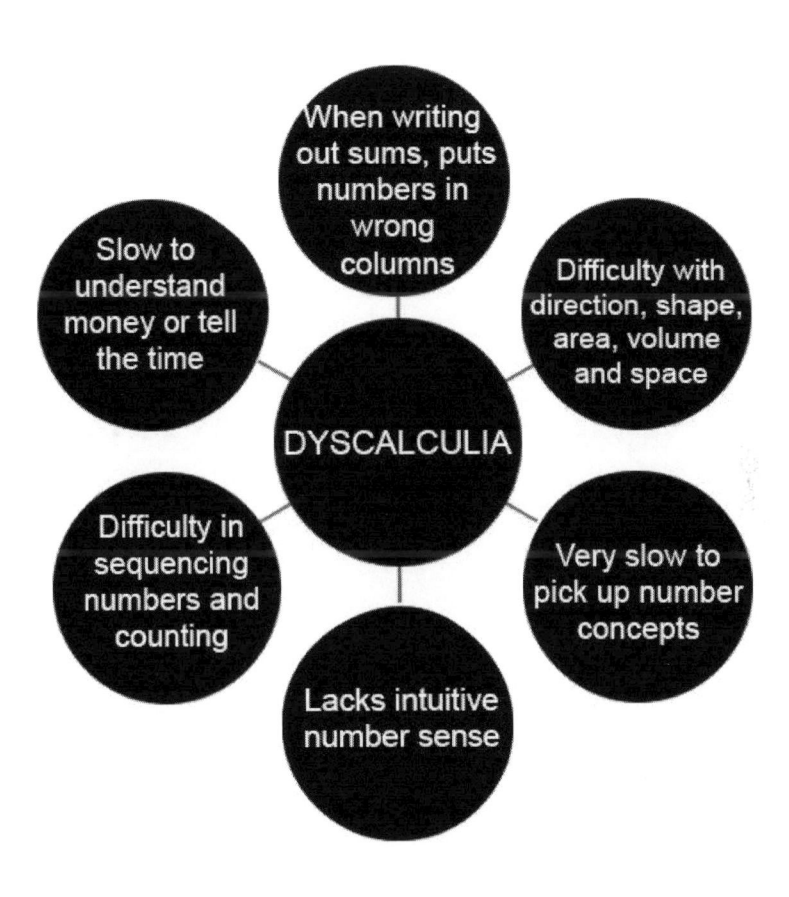

```
              When writing
              out sums, puts
                numbers in
                  wrong
   Slow to        columns
  understand                  Difficulty with
  money or tell                direction, shape,
   the time                    area, volume
                               and space

              DYSCALCULIA

  Difficulty in
  sequencing                  Very slow to
  numbers and                 pick up number
   counting                     concepts

                Lacks intuitive
                number sense
```

Numbers

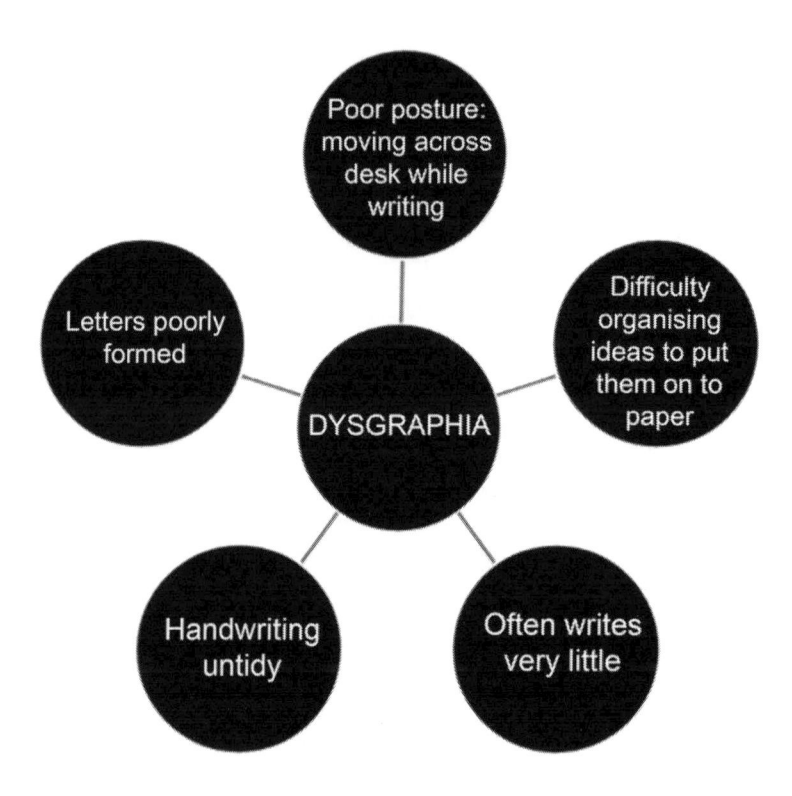

```
                    Poor posture:
                    moving across
                    desk while
                    writing

  Letters poorly                      Difficulty
  formed                              organising
                                      ideas to put
                    DYSGRAPHIA        them on to
                                      paper

        Handwriting           Often writes
        untidy                very little
```

Letters

DYSNOMIA

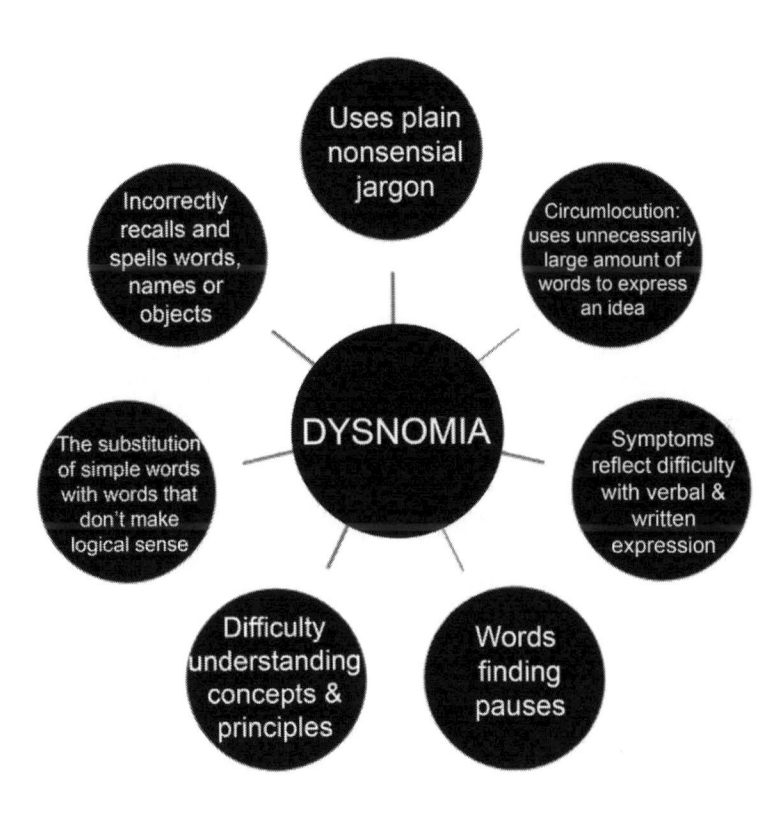

- Uses plain nonsensial jargon
- Circumlocution: uses unnecessarily large amount of words to express an idea
- Symptoms reflect difficulty with verbal & written expression
- Words finding pauses
- Difficulty understanding concepts & principles
- The substitution of simple words with words that don't make logical sense
- Incorrectly recalls and spells words, names or objects

Take a simple task like asking a child with ADHD to complete a piece of homework for a subject they dislike or find difficult. Even with just one of the above-mentioned learning difficulties, the child will also possibly experience a fear of failure (atychiphobia), which in my opinion is a permeating symptom of ADHD.

- Lacks trust in grown-ups,
- Worries about understanding
- Anxious about being made to look stupid
- Insecure, uncertain and may tend to avoid situations they fear failure at
- Has a self-defeating attitude
- May subconsciously undermine their own efforts so that they no longer have to continue to try.
- Can be ambivalent and has a tendency to project his feelings of failure onto others.

Atichyphobia

The child may experience frustration at the thought of having to concentrate, which will generate anxiety about the task itself, and the amount of time they are expected to take over it. This will often be expressed as anger, which will then accelerate their (emotional and possibly physical) hyperactivity. What goes up must come down, so this heightened state eventually descends into a low mood which may be permeated by feelings of shame, guilt, and embarrassment. This cycle can create a depressing mood of a fear of failure.

Depression → Frustration → Anxiety → Discontent → Hyperactivity / Overthinking → Depression

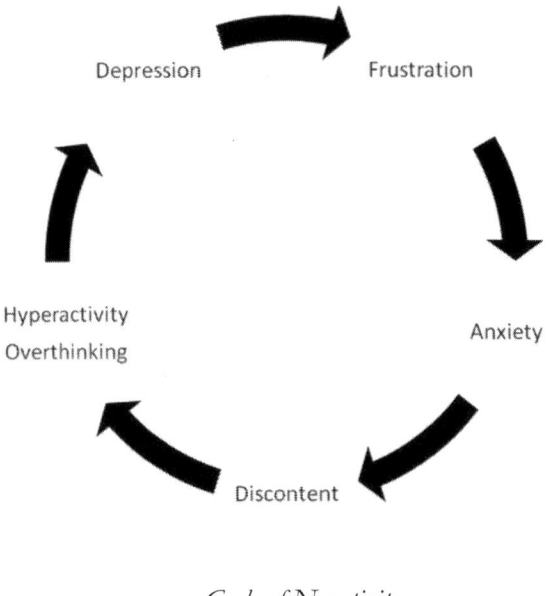

Cycle of Negativity

A major challenge to improve support for children with ADHD is to establish an accurate and full diagnosis for each individual, given that confusion often frustrates attempts to differentiate ADHD and other conditions when there is a high rate of co-morbidity between them.

It is also quite difficult to assess teenagers, as some of their symptoms can apply to the processes of normal pubescent development. This can make it difficult to determine which behaviours might suggest a disability as symptoms like irritability, disorganisation and mood swings are a common part of adolescence. However if symptoms are reported to occur to such a degree that they impair functioning, this may indicate more than just the stress of being a 'teenager'.

On the subject of age progression, some people think that people with ADHD find it easier to cope as they get older. My view is that as they get older people with ADHD can find it even harder to cope.

Society is less accepting of different behaviours and people with ADHD do try their hardest to conform and be accepted. In doing so, they suppress or disguise a lot of their natural presentations. This unfortunately places them under additional stress. Eventually they will reach their breaking point, and this can result in depression, social anxiety, and in some cases, agoraphobia.

As one moves through the transitional stages of life, there are increasing expectations from others. Also, remember that ADHD presentations are erratic in nature, so one can never predict how one is going to feel, behave, or react on a given day to a particular set of circumstances. Added to this is the fact that people with ADHD tend to act and feel much younger than their chronological age... and the frustrations of fitting in are often overwhelmed by the never-ending all-consuming fear of failure. Thus, societal milestones may not be achieved on time due to the child being too immature or not having learned the appropriate behaviours for their chronological age. This can generate anxiety that is often consoled with addictions like alcohol, tobacco, cannabis, gambling and sex.

It is of course, essential to recognise that levels of these ADHD and ancillary symptoms will vary from child to child, and one must not assume that one child has the same generalised symptoms as all the others.

It is also important to identify and understand the differences between ADHD and ADD (ADHD inattentive type) as the presentations are very unalike. Often where there is a dual diagnosis, support tends to focus on addressing the ADHD behaviours because these are socially unacceptable. Consequently, the other condition is often overlooked and the emotional impact of this can be developmentally detrimental.

Here are some of the different characteristics displayed by two children with ADHD:

ADHD: REFLECTIONS ON A HIDDEN DISABILITY

10 year old girl. Diagnosed with ADHD

- Lacks empathy
- Can hyper focus when motivated
- Kind and considerate
- Blunt sense of humor
- Visual learner. Creative imagination
- Hypersensitive to criticism
- Talks to herself and to objects (i.e. a chair)
- Says whatever pops into her head
- 'Blanks out' and is difficult to re-engage
- Answers back has to have the last word

Child 1

8 year old boy. Diagnosed with ADHD

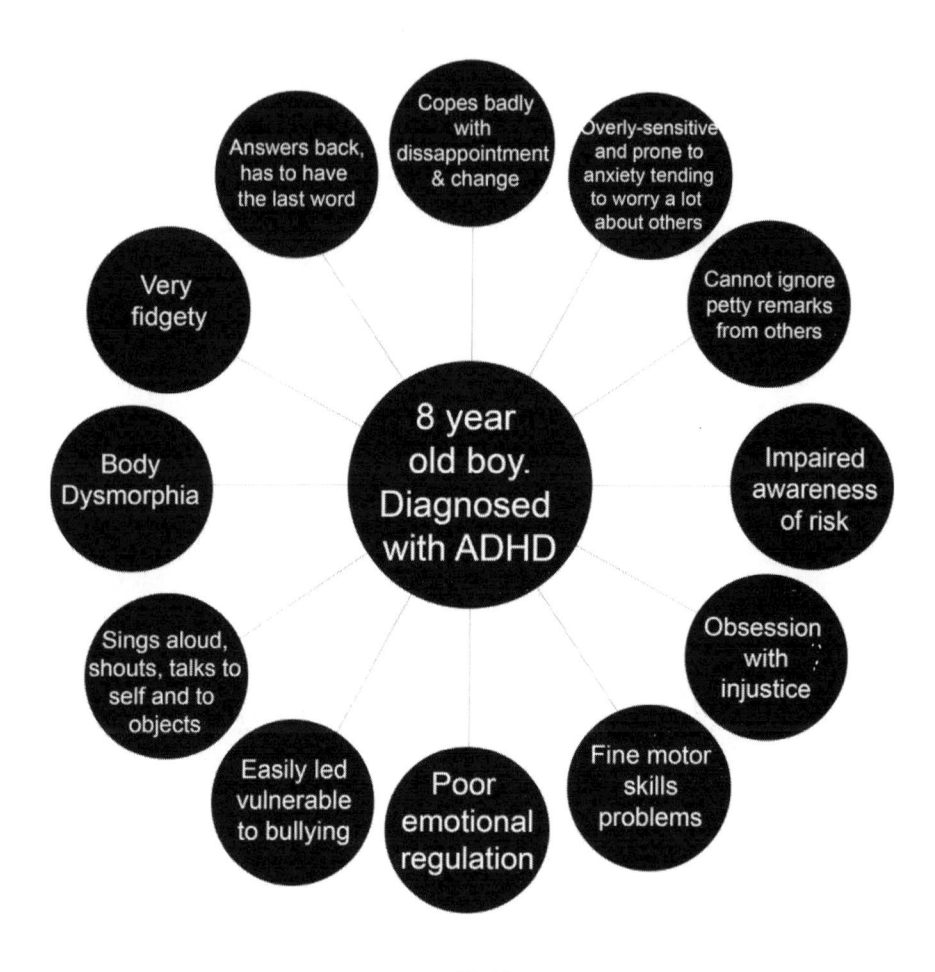

- Answers back, has to have the last word
- Copes badly with dissappointment & change
- Overly-sensitive and prone to anxiety tending to worry a lot about others
- Cannot ignore petty remarks from others
- Impaired awareness of risk
- Obsession with injustice
- Fine motor skills problems
- Poor emotional regulation
- Easily led vulnerable to bullying
- Sings aloud, shouts, talks to self and to objects
- Body Dysmorphia
- Very fidgety

Child 2

Chapter 3

Parent Experiences

These days everyone knows someone who has ADHD, and opinions are varied and subjective.

* Some people detest and disparage and therefore cause damage.
* Some people try to change and cure and therefore exert control.
* Some people accept and assist and therefore help advance ADHD. This is the most progressive way forward.

If you accept the diagnosis and disability label then you can positively assist the child and advance their development. This may sound like a simplistic view but it is a mental processing task. **If you view it as a disability, it will disable you. If you view it as a difference, it will empower you.**

What parents and professionals say about ADHD depends on what they know, learn and do. Parents want practical information, guidance and support. However, they should know that without a better understanding of the condition they will inadvertently be contributing to the cycle of negativity that surrounds children with ADHD.

The difficult behaviours and the peculiar presentations of children with ADHD push people away, so social exclusion is often experienced from a very early age. Excluded from birthday parties, school lunchtimes and school trips, playtimes, PE sessions, social clubs, shopping trips, holiday clubs, family events...

The parents of these children also face the same exclusion:

> I've got no friends left

> What must the neighbours think!

> Why did this happen to me?

> I feel angry & depressed

> I can't take much more of this!

Imagine the following:

* Constantly having to apologise to your neighbours over noise levels, offensive language or damage etc. is tiresome.

* Having to collect your child early from school.

* Being ignored or screamed at in the playground. Being stared at and criticised in the supermarket.

* Blamed by family members or told off by teachers.

* The implication from all of this negativity is that you begin to feel like you are failing as a parent, and it is your entire fault and that society is judging you.

Parents of a child with ADHD may not have access to any form of respite, so the time their children spend at school is their only free time. You may realise that you have started to become isolated. As your child gets older and goes to nursery or school, you suddenly start getting daily phone calls from the staff to collect your child early. When you go in the next day, other parents stare at you in the playground. Some may even confront you, accusing you of being a bad parent who can't control their unruly or violent child. Other children start to avoid your child and they are often instructed to do so by their parents, who also avoid you in the playground, where you are singled out by your child's teacher. You start to become anxious about taking your child to school. Whether you spend the day at work or at home, you'll remain worried, and anticipate being called to collect your child early. Parents often say they dread the phone ringing.

Invitations to your child's peers' birthday parties cease. Friends stop inviting you to social events because they dislike your child's behaviours. Isolation sets in as you start to feel judged and become resentful. As parents you are more stressed and can start to blame each other. If you're not on your own, this can become a looming possibility as your personal relationship deteriorates. You stop going out and may even develop an anxiety condition or depression; you feel a sense of futility – of helplessness and hopelessness. You seek support but it is very limited.

You may be offered the choice of medicating your child. This may well help to some degree in school but when the medication wears off after school, your child is like a whirlwind. Nothing seems to work for long. You feel a sense of desperation, of guilt, of frustration... This is even worse if you are a lone parent, as parents of a child with ADHD have very little time and energy for a meaningful, enduring relationship.

Parental isolation can become a cycle of emotional burden.

Depression → Guilt / Shame → Anger → Rejection → Isolation → Social Anxiety → Depression

This is the life that other people don't see in total. They may see parts of your life and may even offer a degree of sympathy, but the reality is that you are on your own. No one really understands, not the teachers, the doctors, the siblings, the family, least of all your child with ADHD.

What I can tell you is that you are not alone. But let us remember here, you are the grown-up; if it is this difficult for you, imagine what it is like for the child.

Your child is a square peg that you and everyone else are trying to fit into a round hole. Well… stop right now! If we accept that society has a right to be protected from children and young people with perceived difficult conduct, then children and young people with ADHD have a right to protection from the inequalities and the prejudices of adult society.

Being and feeling different in a neuro-typical world is difficult. More so because often the lives of children with ADHD can be blighted with deprivation, disaffection, de-motivation, disappointment, degradation, and dismissal. Often their world becomes filled with the complaints from grown-ups, whose need to control leads to labelling the children's behaviours as negative. So there is a real need to understand and accept the ADHD experiences and perceptions of the children and young people as genuine.

As a parent of a child with ADHD you may not realise it but, you are actually a specialist! You are the one with all the knowledge and information about your child's condition, its presentation, and the most effective support strategies. Everyone else who gets involved to assess, support, teach your child needs information from you. Even the doctors who treat the child need your expertise. Accept this as a fact; you are the expert authority on your child. You are an ADHD Specialist!

As a parent, you may have managed to get a diagnosis for your child, and you will most probably be given a factsheet and possibly some pills and sent on your way. There is, however, an upside: you have a child who is different, which makes you and the child special.

In an ideal world there would be much better support services for families with ADHD.

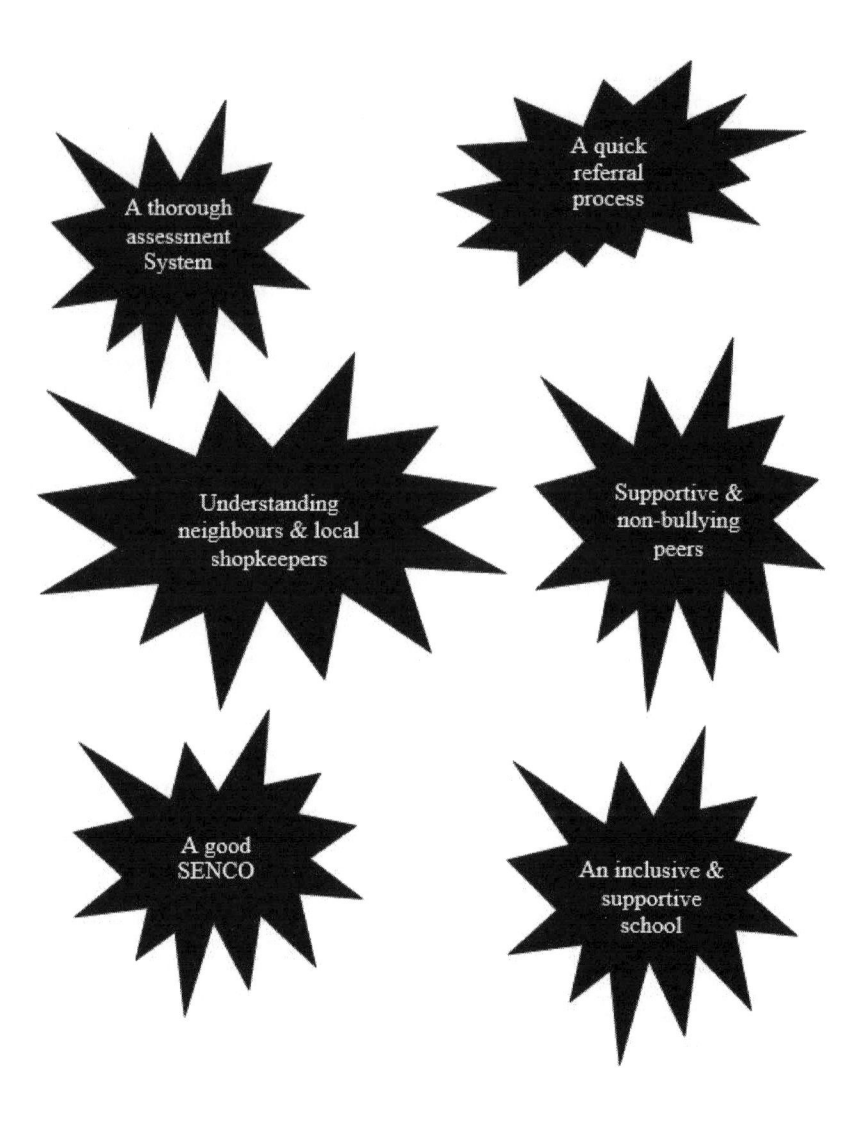

- A thorough assessment System
- A quick referral process
- Understanding neighbours & local shopkeepers
- Supportive & non-bullying peers
- A good SENCO
- An inclusive & supportive school

The above, are however, hard to find, especially as we live in a world where hidden disabilities are often dismissed or misunderstood. So if you have any of these then you are indeed lucky.

Chapter 4

Child Experiences

From a very early age children with ADHD are surrounded by a cycle of negativity. Adverse reactions and feedback which these pupils receive from their social surroundings because of their difficulties, creates a Cycle of Negativity that facilitates conflict and reinforces the lack of acceptance they feel. This can promote adverse resilience. The cycle of negativity often starts with parents. No parent does this deliberately but they are under pressure from family members, neighbours, nursery and school staff, child minders, etc. to ensure that their child fits in. So they try their best to make the child conform to the expectations of other adults.

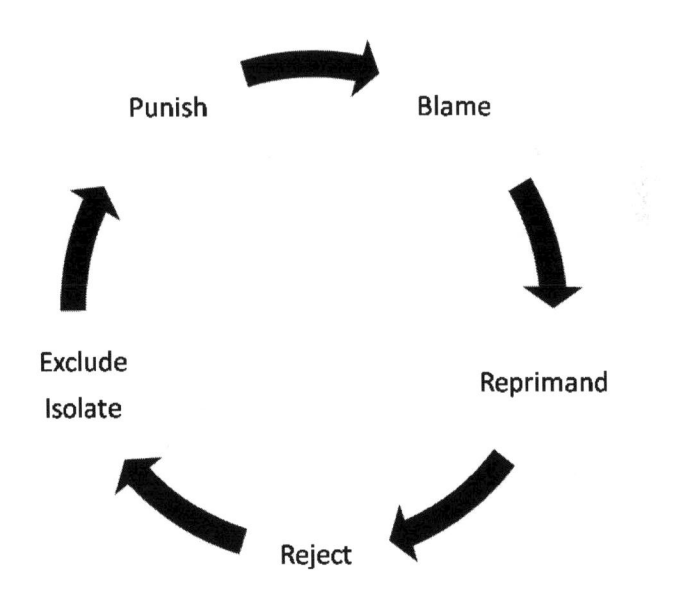

Punish → Blame → Reprimand → Reject → Exclude Isolate → Punish

What Adults Do

Anger → Frustration → Anxiety → Rejection → Fear of Failure → (Anger)

What Children Feel

As a parent or teacher, you may find yourself commanding the child with ADHD to sit still; stop shouting; stop making strange noises and sounds; stop picking up or fiddling with objects.

You may find yourself pulling them away from other children when they poke, trip, grab, or hit them.

You may scold the child for being clumsy or for not paying attention.

You may shout at them for being too loud or too quiet, or for blurting out inappropriate statements or for using swear words, etc.

How many times have you found yourself shouting out the following negative statements?

ADHD: REFLECTIONS ON A HIDDEN DISABILITY

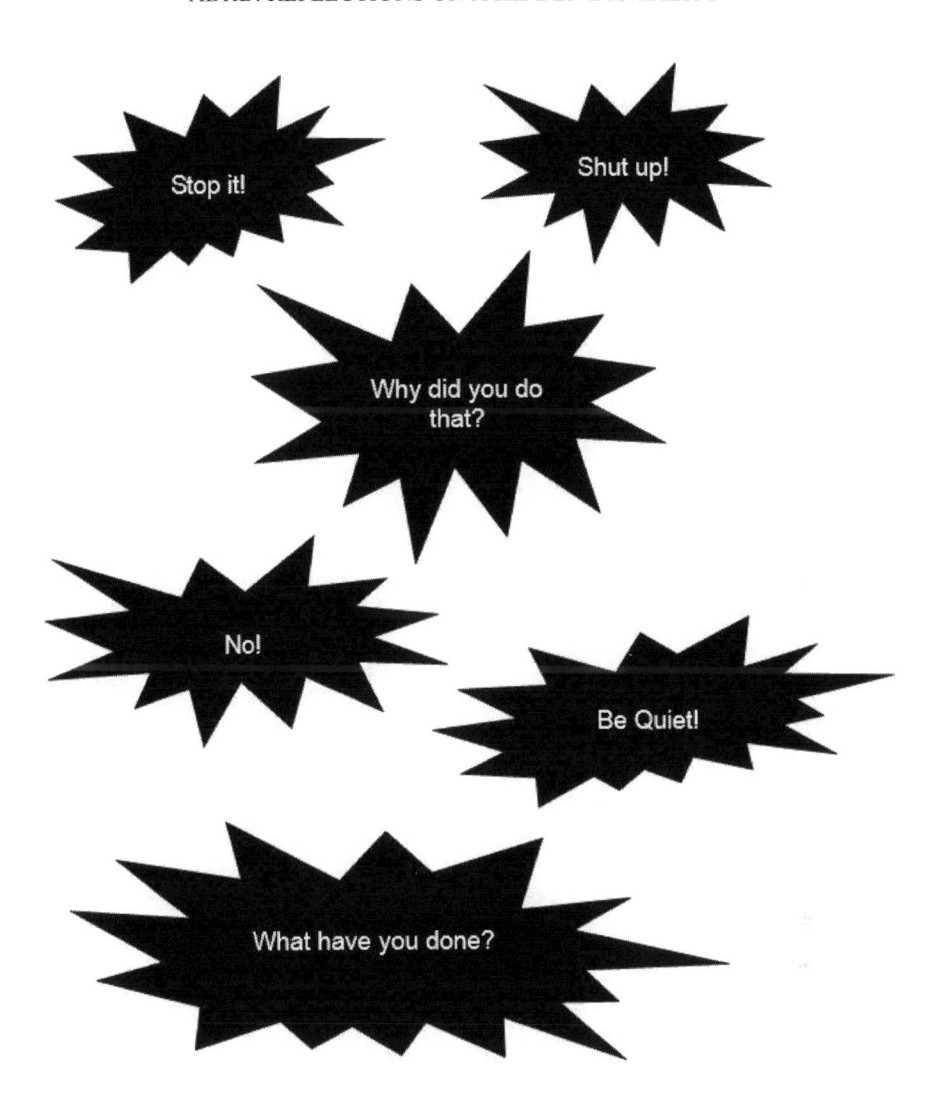

- Stop it!
- Shut up!
- Why did you do that?
- No!
- Be Quiet!
- What have you done?

Here are some more negative labels used by parents and teachers to describe the behaviours of a child with ADHD:

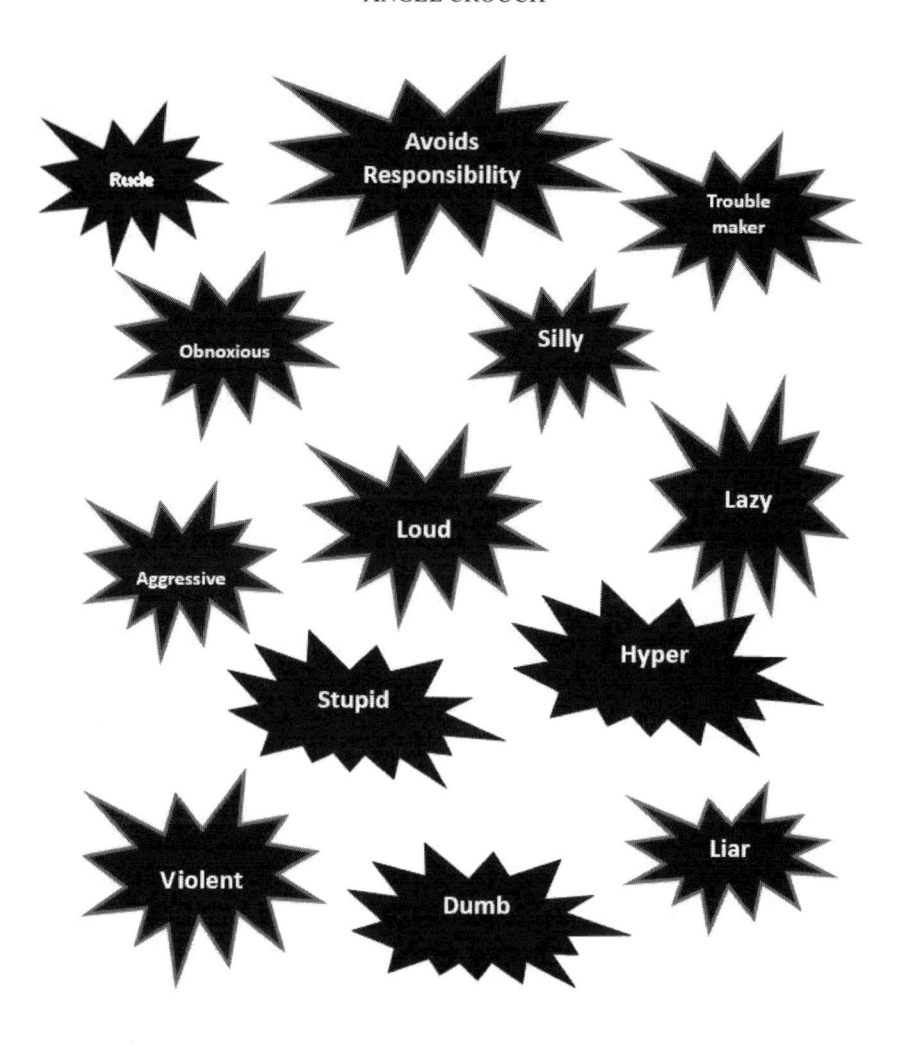

Rude
Avoids Responsibility
Trouble maker
Obnoxious
Silly
Aggressive
Loud
Lazy
Stupid
Hyper
Violent
Dumb
Liar

Take a moment to imagine the overall effect of constantly being demoralised and intimidated.

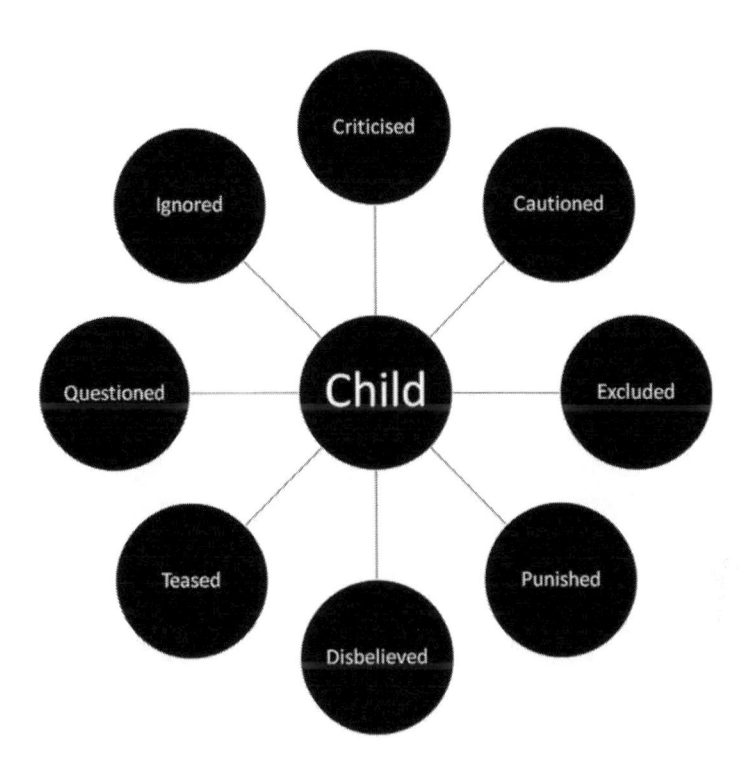

Diagram: A central circle labeled "Child" is surrounded by eight circles labeled: Criticised, Cautioned, Excluded, Punished, Disbelieved, Teased, Questioned, Ignored.

How do you think you might react to constantly experiencing some of the above?

Unfortunately it is often the child with ADHD who gets accused of bullying others. In my experience, this is due to the cumulative effect of the irritating and frustratingly difficult to endure nature of some of their presentations. People simply get fed up and as we all know, repetitive irritation leads to frustration and consequent stress which then leads to loss of control. What is really interesting here is that often, adults become guilty of behaving in the same way as the children with ADHD – shouting, blaming, overreacting, unconscious persecuting. The list of negatives applied to children with ADHD is endless. But the significance of the cycle of negativity and its impact on a child cannot be dismissed as it can lead to increased states of the following cycle of negative emotions:

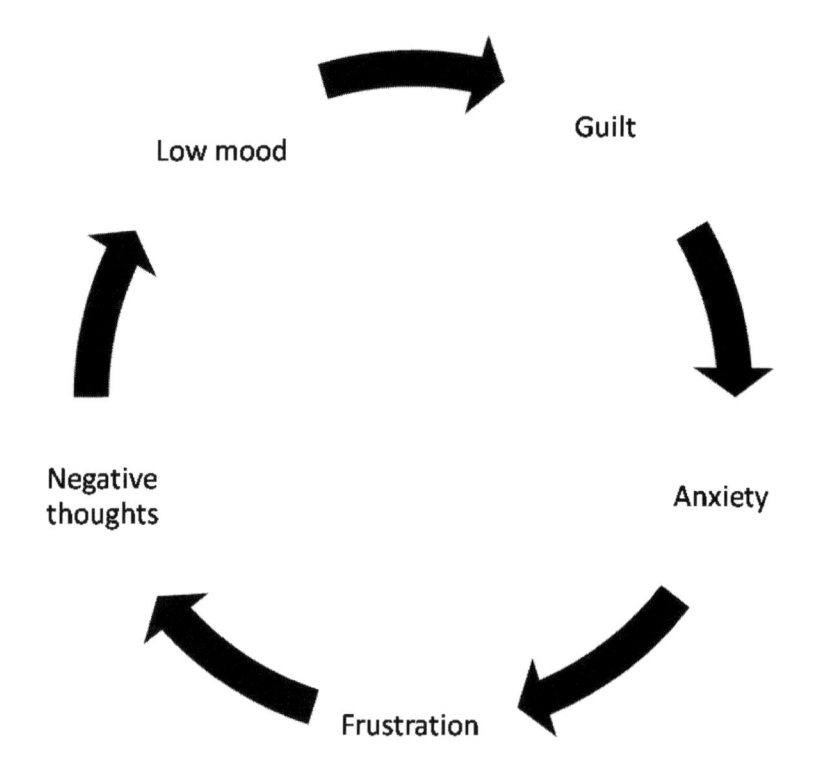

```
        Low mood  →  Guilt
           ↑            ↓
  Negative thoughts    Anxiety
           ↖            ↙
             Frustration
```

Consider hearing just one of these negative statements several times a day – before school, during school, after school, at weekends. One eleven-year-old boy with a diagnosis of ADHD and ODD told me that he is often reprimanded and criticised in his dreams.

Here are some examples of what children have said about their actual experiences:

> I can't help touching things and people.

> I make noises cos I'm anxious. Then I get told off and make even more noises. So I get told off again and again for the same thing.

> People say they understand ADHD but they don't understand me.

> Why do I always get the blame?

> Nobody ever believes me when I say I don't know why I did it.

> I guess I've got used to being called stupid.

Children with ADHD will often be labelled as having behavioural difficulties. These children can become desensitised and hard-hearted due to all these negative responses they receive. Their ability to empathise is pre-set below the normal threshold, and the adverse experiences and inadvertent rejections which they frequently receive can create perceived oppositional defiance, that may well be a reaction to being fed up of hearing negative comments about their behaviour all the time, and being and feeling punished.

Unfortunately, this is a vicious circle. The child's negative behaviour warrants challenging, and challenging the negative behaviour causes opposition and defiance. This situation is worsened by the fact that their ADHD and/or ancillary difficulties cause them to have a resistance to taking responsibility for their behaviours, and a predisposition to deflect blame onto someone else. This may also be due to their unrealistic and rigid sense of perceived injustice and their perceptions of other peoples' actions that they think are unfair. They also have a low tolerance for frustration and may have an urge to punish others for their own unhappy feelings. This can stimulate vengeful bullying behaviours.

Children with ADHD exhibit very strong emotional reactions, so little things often provoke a disproportionately dramatic response. A child may seek to empower themselves by arguing with adults as a defence against their feelings of powerlessness. So unconsciously, they use these conflicts as an outlet for their inner frustrations and anger. So the more you push, the angrier the child may get. Children with ADHD are quick to show defiance and display an unrealistic sense of justice when things do go wrong. They may point out the poor behaviour of others and tend to become angry at what they perceive to be injustices.

Children with ADHD do know what to do and how to behave but in the heat of a moment, their sense of instant need can override their flawed capacity for self-discipline. Thus, their behaviour might be inconsistent and unpredictable – difficult to anticipate from moment to moment. Sometimes they may behave appropriately and adults will wonder why they can't do this all the time. So adults may become more punitive in disciplining the child.

Premeditation is not usually a factor in young people with ADHD for they act on impulse and do not utilise the capacity to think in terms of 'actions equals consequence'. It is therefore reasonable to consider whether their disability may have contributed in part to issues where the specific incident requires proof of intent. E.g., a child may make noises because they are anxious or embarrassed. This is something the child cannot control and so they should not be reprimanded nor punished for it. They need help identifying the cause of the anxiety or embarrassment. They should be supported to become more mindful of how their noises can have an impact on others.

Remember that if a child frequently experiences too many negative feelings then these can become comforting in the absence of an equal number of positive feelings. Consequently, the child may start to consciously act in a negative manner to provoke those negative-turned-positive feelings.

Chapter 5

The Different Approach

Parents of children with ADHD or most disabilities are resilient, intuitive and informed about their child's condition. However, subject to how socially embarrassed by their child's behaviour they are or how much they are caught up in the cycles of negativity, they are inclined to do all they can to make their square peg child fit into the round hole of 'average' society.

Parents tend to feel compelled to try and make their child fit into the neuro-typical world in order to avoid being subjected to blame or embarrassment.

Consequently they do all they can to try and stop their child from behaving in a way that is natural for them, thereby curtailing their child's free will i.e. reprimanding them for making noises that we consider inappropriate, but for the child with ADHD is their compulsive form of expression and communication.

A more vivid example of the culture of negativity is when exclusion takes place. For instance, when a child is excluded from school they may experience along with this sanction: the humiliation of being taken out of a lesson, the social exclusion of having to wait outside the head teacher's room or school office, and then having to explain what happened to other staff and pupils.

The child's anxiety will further increase as they will fret about their parent's reaction. Then you (parent) arrive on the scene to collect your child. You may possibly already be fuming at having to come to the school, having suffered the embarrassment of having had a call put through at work from the school. Gosh, some of your work colleagues are now aware that your child is in trouble at school. You may, on the other hand, have been enjoying your one moment of free time or doing the things you've put off doing because of your child's behaviours. The bottom line is that when you arrive at school, you are seething and worried about the consequences of the exclusion.

You then have to endure a telling off from a teacher who, inadvertently, is demeaning your parenting skills. This is both hurtful and humiliating. Yet despite these negative feelings, you feel compelled to go along with the school's approach and may consequently further chastise your child in spite of all the negativity the child has already suffered.

So no matter how angry you feel when you get your child home, don't punish them again or else how is the child supposed to be able to separate what you do from what the school does? If you act in the same way then this is impossible.

In order to make positive changes, parents need to go through the range of negative emotions associated with ADHD, but finally accepting the diagnosis and seeing it as a difference rather than a disability can be enabling.

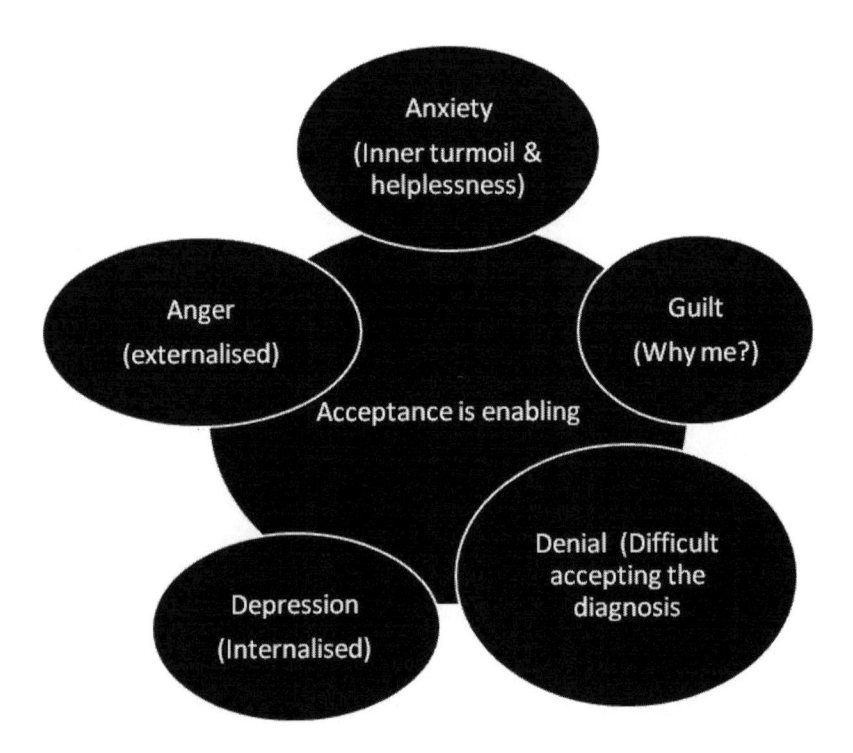

- Anxiety (Inner turmoil & helplessness)
- Anger (externalised)
- Guilt (Why me?)
- Denial (Difficult accepting the diagnosis)
- Depression (Internalised)

Acceptance is enabling

Chapter 6

Commonalities and Consideration

There are several manifestations of ADHD which seem to be common among children and adults. I am not making excuses. I just want you to understand that for people with ADHD, these manifestations are to be expected. It is therefore important to consider putting their behaviours and presentations into situational context when issues arise. It will help if you make such reasonable adjustments as are appropriate and necessary. My repeated use of the words 'people with ADHD' is deliberate as I want you to remember them.

It is common for people with ADHD to experience negativity on a daily basis because they don't look disabled and they consequently face scepticism and stigma.

It is common for people with ADHD to talk fast, mumble, and quickly forget whatever it was they said.

It is common for people with ADHD to experience mood swings and impulsive anger, with the particular reason for the specific behaviours presented not being easily identifiable. Mood swings can come completely out of the blue with no reason at all, occurring within the mind from nowhere.

It is common for people with ADHD to lack tolerance but unfortunately this can make them appear as selfish and uncaring of others' needs.

It is common for people with ADHD to struggle to manage unpredictable situations or changes to their expectations and routines.

It is common for people with ADHD to make noises or have vocal 'tics'. It's like a compulsive need to release a bit of energy.

It is common for people with ADHD to experience difficulty appreciating thoughts, feelings and opinions of other people, as they tend not to be able to think about others in this way.

It is common for people with ADHD to interrupt a lot, complete the sentences of others, and talk at a very fast pace. It is often difficult to discern whether this is due to being impulsive – a need to say everything in one go, to avoid forgetting anything, or a deficit in understanding the social nuances of conversation. It could be a combination of all of the above.

It is common for people with ADHD to have narrow-minded perceptions. It is important to understand that the inability to see things from another's point of view or to put oneself in the shoes of another is not reluctance. It is simply very difficult because the ADHD brain inhibits normal processing. People with ADHD tend to have obsessive thoughts and therefore cannot consider several different views or opinions at once.

It is common for people with ADHD to seek power and control as a self-protective measure when they feel events are spiralling out of control or when they perceive or experience intense anxiety.

It is common for people with ADHD to have a reduced ability to understand the social interactions around them, so rage may have become a pattern of behaviour for them to maintain a sense of control and familiarity in a world which feels chaotic and illogical.

It is common for people with ADHD to indulge in self-talk. Others find this odd. But it helps subjects to verbalise their thoughts and sometimes this can help them select a particular thought. Sounding it out loud allows them to focus better and inhibit other sensory distractions.

It is common for people with ADHD to have very extreme mood swings. Some children with ADHD have described these moments as scary, as they seem to lose control for no apparent reason. This can be momentary explosions of rage that last from a few seconds to several minutes, and are then followed by a low moment where they then struggle to understand what just occurred. Sometimes they may not even remember it.

It is common for people with ADHD to experience criticism, feel inadequate, overwhelmed, and pessimistic about their future. They may consequently experience low moods that can deteriorate into depression. The levels of depression can be worsened by their daily experiences of negativity. Depression can also make their concentration worse, so making good decisions or choices becomes even harder.

It is common for people with ADHD to repeatedly experience self-doubt because they have a fear that they will fail at something, so they avoid trying at all. Better to get out of doing something rather than go through the negative cycle of experiencing anxiety, frustration and then worst of all, the public embarrassment that they perceive they will suffer when they make themselves look stupid yet again. Even when they do something well, it's hard for them to accept that it wasn't luck because they may have become so used to others excluding them from participation or doubting their commitment to conform to a set of rules.

It is common for people to tell a child with ADHD how badly they behave, so it is therefore common for children with ADHD to fail to acknowledge positives about their lives. They may start to believe it to be true; that they are bad and a failure, and so they often have low self-esteem.

It is common for people with ADHD to refuse to accept that other people's views should be considered as reasonable. So they will be dissatisfied with the manner in which parents and teachers deal with, or resolve conflicts. Accordingly, they will complain about being treated unfairly and believe the world is unjust and stacked against them, and this can build up resentment against individual adults.

It is common for people with ADHD to demonstrate a narrow focus in both thought and action, where they are unable to consider other perspectives or behaviours outside those with which they are accustomed. The tendency towards black and white thinking may result in unrealistic choices and perspectives and lead to conflict at home and school. For example, not only may a child believe that their parents should have no control over them, they may also feel that they should control their parents. For that child, any deviation from this means the fear of not being in control which will lead to anxiety and consequently, panic and anger.

It is common for people with ADHD to challenge anything they perceive to be unfair. They cannot help this as they have a strong sense of justice, and impulsivity can make their expressions appear blunt or insulting... They may also find any challenge to their perception of events difficult to handle and this can result in conflict. So by default, people with ADHD will be more argumentative and dissenting. This mind-set does not sit well in schools or the workplace.

It is common for people with ADHD to adopt persistent negative thinking or imagination. This can become a coping strategy; they adopt to deal with situations that make them anxious, like starting a task at school. Avoiding starting this task prevents another experience of failure which further dents the self-esteem. So embracing despondency can become a self-fulfilling prophecy. "If I try, I will fail" becomes "I will fail so I won't try". A teacher may refer to such behaviours as lazy and demotivated.

It is common for people with ADHD (especially those who also have autistic traits) to replay events they have seen and heard in their head and put themselves back into that situation and dialogue it out. They may start laughing at the funny parts or get upset by the sad parts. Sometimes they may experience literal auditory recall incidences and hear the replay as voices rather than thoughts.

It is common for children with ADHD to have some difficulties with spatial awareness, so often they can appear clumsy and tend to bump into things or people. They may not be aware of what is appropriate personal space and will therefore invade this inadvertently, i.e. standing too close or too far away from the person they are relating to. They may lean in as they lose balance or they may rock from side to side without even being aware of it.

It is common for people with ADHD to present as younger than their chronological age. They often tend to get on better with younger children and this can cause difficulties with their peer group.

It is common for children with ADHD to have some visual perceptual difficulties. This may indicate the presence of a more specific learning difficulty such as dyslexia or dyspraxia. They may become confused when they try to work out direction from instructions such as push/pull in/out, over/under, vertical/horizontal, and North, South, East and West. This deficit also impacts on understanding abstract concepts like volume, space, shapes, area, length, and breadth.

It is common for people with ADHD to make lists of people whom they dislike or against whom they seek revenge. For some these are mere hate lists and the vengeful action will never happen. For some others, the notion of revenge can become an obsession fuelled by the pain felt about a perceived injustice. This should not be taken lightly.

One cannot underestimate the intensity of individual difficulties people with ADHD can experience. Yet unfortunately, their presentations and behaviours are too often viewed as problems and labelled as non-conforming. The reality is that the sorts of issues described here are very much normal for individuals with a brain difference.

Chapter 7
ADHD Voices

> "One of the things that makes me really angry is when I think someone has criticised me. Sometimes they don't even have to say anything. I can see it in the way they look at me. This winds me up something big and my mind starts plotting straight away about how to get them back. Sometimes I can't think about anything else and therefore don't even hear someone else calling me. When I am in this mode the only way to get my attention is not by shouting at me or poking me, but by approaching me from the front. If you shout at me or touch me, I will probably react with aggression without realising it."
>
> – 15 year old boy (Diagnosis: ADHD)

"We've got football today and I'm no good at it. The coach says I've no skill and lack coordination. I also fall over a lot. So I always get shouted at by the coach and mocked by the other pupils. I used to think I was okay at sports but now I doubt my own abilities. I've had about as much of it as I can take so now, I avoid going altogether. I've deliberately hidden my PE kit so I don't have to participate in the lesson.   Less stress! I guess it's a coping strategy of sorts."

-14 year old boy (Diagnosis: ADHD)

"I often have trouble filtering different sounds. For instance, in my class which is always loud, I sometimes can't distinguish the teacher's voice from those of other children in the class. Then I get accused of not following instructions. When I try to explain, no one believes me... It is easier to bunk school than put up with being told off and shouted at daily."

-16 year old girl diagnosis ADHD

"No one will play with me. I wish I had a best friend."

-7 year old boy (Diagnosis ADHD and Dysgraphia)

"I always forget what I'm supposed to remember. I can't help it. I really do try and remember things but it doesn't work. Everyone shouts at me: Mum calls me a Goldfish; other kids call me stupid and they're always laughing at me, One teacher picks on me all the time, asking me questions cos he knows I won't remember the answers. He does it to show me up cos everyone laughs. So I got fed up with feeling like a stupid dickhead having the piss taken out of me every day. School makes me feel stupid and I hate it."

-15 year old boy (Diagnosis ADHD)

"I'm bad...I'm always bad. Everyone says it, even when I try hard to behave, people still shout at me so what's the point of being good?"

-9 year old boy (Diagnosis ADHD)

"I try to sleep but my brain won't stop talking to itself."

-8 year old boy (Diagnosis ADHD)

"I often do stupid things like stick my leg out and trip someone over as they walk by me, or throw something at someone for no reason. I don't really know why, it just happens. The worst part is when adults ask me why I did it and I tell them I don't know. They never believe me and the more they ask me why, the angrier I get cos I really don't know."

-14 year old boy (Diagnosis ADHD)

"I hate brushing my teeth. My mum thinks I'm being defiant but I'm not. I don't like the feel of the brush in my mouth. Sometimes I think the brush is going to slip down my throat and choke me. I know it is unlikely to happen but it doesn't stop me worrying about it."

-12 year old boy diagnosis: ADHD & Aspergers

"All I want is to be a little bit happier and not feel that everyone hates me because I've got ADHD."

-10 year old boy diagnosed with ADHD

"What really winds me up is when people shout or use a sarcastic voice in speaking to me. I'll either get really angry or ignore them completely. Either way I always end up in trouble."

-14 year old boy (Diagnosis ADHD & Dyslexia)

"I can't help using rude words. They just sort of pop into my head and my mouth. I don't mean to offend people with what I say but that is just what happens. People say I'm insensitive and racist; but I'm not. Nowadays, I don't go out so I don't get into trouble."

-15 year old boy (Diagnosis ADHD & depression)

"I seem to get blamed for things that I haven't even done. One day the school called my mum to come and collect me. They said a group of us students were being excluded for unruly and rude behaviour and that I had sworn at a teacher. I wasn't even in school that day as I was sick. This really upset my mum. The next day I did go to school and asked the teacher to apologise for getting it wrong. He refused so I swore at him and got excluded. How is that fair?"

-15 year old boy (Diagnosis ADHD)

> When incidents happen and I tell the teachers, they don't do anything and then sometimes they accuse me of lying and then they bring up things that happened a long time ago. Nowadays I don't bother telling, I just try and sort it out myself."
>
> -10 year old boy (Diagnosis ADHD)

> "Often I don't trust myself because I have a fear that I will fail at something so I avoid trying. Better to get out of something rather than start worrying about whether I'll be able to do it."
>
> -12 year old boy (Diagnosis ADHD)

> If you're shouting then I'm probably not listening!"
>
> - 11 year old girl (Diagnosis ADHD)

"I swear a lot cos I can't usually think of words that will describe how angry I feel. Sometimes though, swear words just come out of my mouth for no reason."

-11 year old boy (Diagnosis ADHD)

"I have a habit of making weird sounds when things are too quiet. I don't know why, I just do".

-10 year old boy (Diagnosis ADHD)

"I hate school! Teachers are always telling me off."

- 11 year old girl with ADHD and LD

"I'm not lazy. I'm just highly motivated not to do anything I find boring."

-14 year old girl (Diagnosis ADHD)

"When I'm bored, I'm disruptive and self-destructive...I need motivation to behave."
-15 year old girl (Diagnosis ADHD & Dyslexia)

"I keep making the same mistakes over and over again. The teachers are right...I must be stupid."
-13 year old girl Diagnosis ADHD)

"ADHD children are like dogs; if you don't exercise them, they'll wreck your house."
-15 year old boy diagnosed with ADHD, Tourettes & Aspergers

"My mum said I'd be cleverer if I didn't have ADHD."
-7 year old boy diagnosed with ADHD

"What my mum doesn't know is that I cry a lot. Usually when I am reminded how unhappy and lonely I am – which is very often."

-13 year old boy (Diagnosis ADHD)

"I often forget things and when I remember them, the sequence is all messed up. So when I tell it, I get accused of lying."

-15 year old girl (Diagnosis ADHD)

Chapter 8

Top Tips

For children with ADHD and co-morbid conditions, some things are just normal to them and therefore are to be expected. Here is a reminder of some of the more common traits that people without ADHD find frustrating and unusual.

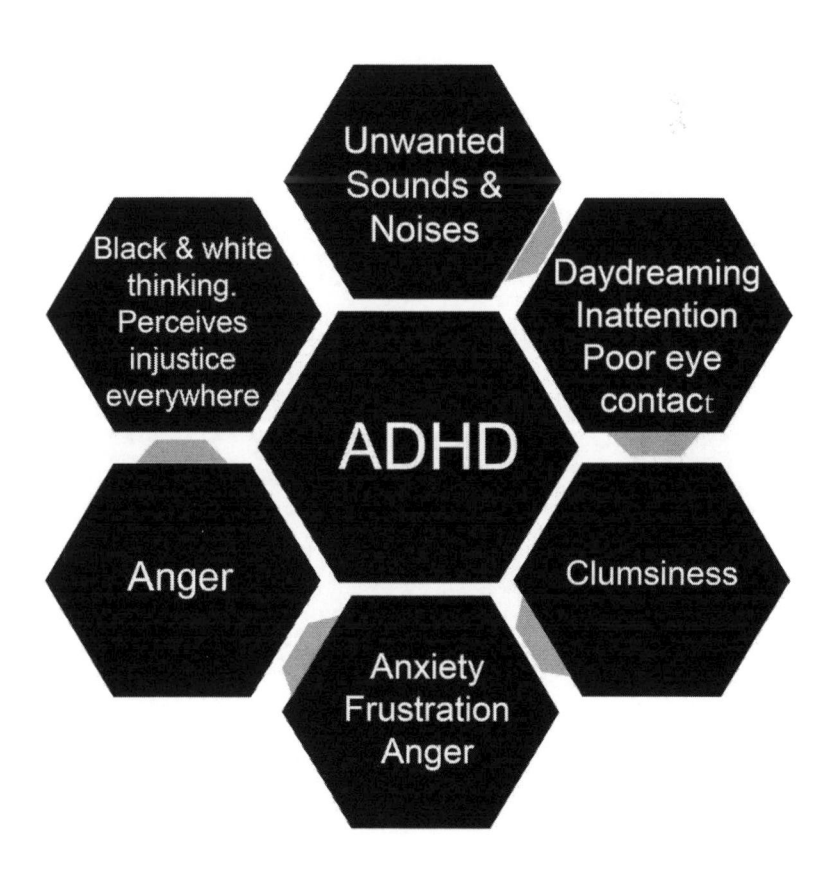

- Unwanted Sounds & Noises
- Black & white thinking. Perceives injustice everywhere
- Daydreaming, Inattention, Poor eye contact
- Anger
- Clumsiness
- Anxiety, Frustration, Anger

Central theme: ADHD

- Instead of telling off, **tell** the child what to do instead.

- Instead of telling the child to stop doing something, **provide** an alternative.

- Create boundaries by **implementing** rewards and consequences.

- Give only **one** instruction at a time. Try to ensure that other grown-ups **use** the same language for instructions.

- Be clear about what you are asking and **demonstrate** it visually if possible.

- A child's short-term memory may be affected by what you say. Long words or words with many syllables are **hard** for them to follow or understand.

- Use **short, specific** words and sentences, and where possible, **enhance** your words with visuals and gestures. It is important not to get carried away and use too many descriptive words to create a picture. Keep it **simple** and be prepared to use the **same** words and phrases **over** and **over** again.

- When a child with ADHD does something wrong, try **not** to ask them **why**. Often, they just don't know why and sometimes, they just can't remember. Asking them why can start a process of annoyance and anger and could lead to the child having a meltdown. This is because previous experiences tell them that you are not going to be satisfied with their answer.

Example:

You: *'Why did you do that?'*

Child: *'I don't know!'*

You: *'You must know.'* (At this point, you're getting angry, which makes the child annoyed because your voice level has probably risen and you are effectively labelling the child a liar.)

When angry, people with ADHD tend to act in a careless manner and won't anticipate the future consequences of their actions.

So, substitute the word 'what' for the word 'why'.

Example:

'What did you do?'

'What are you going to do about it?'

'What will you do to prevent it happening again?'

With ADHD, whatever the presentation, anxiety, anger, aggression, low mood, noises, refusal behaviours, there is always a trigger. Often it may not be that obvious to the child or adult present. It may well be sensory; a reaction to a smell, or sight. It may be a moment of recall from a previous unpleasant memory when the person with ADHD experienced shame, belittlement, and embarrassment that is triggered by a voice, pitch, tone. It may well be a colour or smell that activates an impulsive negative reaction. 'How do you know this is true?' I hear you ask. My answer… how do you know it's not?

Intervene immediately with a prepared strategy such creating as a distraction. If the child is merely annoyed at that stage, you may well be able to prevent annoyance from becoming anger or even worse: fury.

Think about how well you can interpret your child's presentation. How would you know your child is expressing frustration as opposed to expressing anxiety? Can they or you differentiate between signs of fear of failure or anger resulting from a perception of injustice, or resentment or guilt? Does the child even understand more than the literal meanings of the words?

The more you understand about your child's presentation, the easier it will become to identify triggers and prevent escalation of negative presentations.

Think about your child's ADHD more positively. Desist from using negative labels. People with ADHD are also: impetuous, instinctive, intuitive, spontaneous, unpredictable, quirky, unconventional, adventurous, daring, outspoken, bold, not easy to hoodwink, adaptable, loyal, creative, enthusiastic, energetic, inquisitive, resilient, risk-takers, caring, good with younger children and older people (who rarely judge them), quick-witted, and intuitive.

Consistent responses are important but difficult especially if the parent is depressed, 'worn down', or tired after a hard day at work.

Try to think ahead and respond rather than react, i.e., say: "Let's think about how we can make you more comfortable." Instead of saying: "Stop fidgeting/Why can't you sit still?/You're ignoring my instructions again."

ADHD children need mentors. This should be a long-term engagement – setting personal development targets, taking the child out and involving them in the social situations they avoid etc. (I hear and I forget; I see and I remember; I do and I understand).

It's the **'doing'** that will change their thinking, rather than relying solely on the 'thinking' to change their 'doing'. Hope that makes sense.

I have often heard professionals voice their doubts about children diagnosed with ADHD:

"That's not ADHD behaviour."

"We believe the child knew what they were doing."

"They made a choice to misbehave."

"They are choosing when to use their ADHD."

I consider these statements to be ill-informed and discriminatory. If a person has a diagnosis of ADHD then by its very definition, all their behaviours are ADHD behaviours.

When the child is behaving then there are a set of circumstances that create a comfortable environment for that child: motivation, stimulation, sensory.

I believe that children with ADHD do not pick and choose their ADHD moments; they generally try their best but often can't control what comes into their heads or out of their mouths.

They may however tell a lie (deception), to conceal or avoid an uncomfortable situation. For example, a child with ADHD makes a conscious choice to initiate or participate in a misdemeanour (kicked a chair over or swore at a teacher).

There could be many reasons why the child did this: Maybe to get out of the lesson to avoid experiencing failure; maybe a sudden overpowering smell attacked one of their senses; perhaps the tone or pitch of someone's voice generated pain, made them anxious. Maybe the child perceived an attack and got in there first. Maybe the child didn't like the teacher and was getting revenge.

So the next time an educator tells you as a parent: "I don't believe that's ADHD behaviour," ask them how they know it isn't ADHD behaviour.

When children who are on medication miss a dose or stop taking it, their thinking processes may be less restrained and so they will be more likely to perceive unfairness, criticism, and thus experience more perceived negativity which then has a knock on effect of increasing their anxiety.

Recognise that perceived injustices are subjective but very real to the person with ADHD. People with ADHD genuinely believe that their perception of injustice is factual and they will have a logical and plausible argument to back it up. But, this will be a black and white view that will unfortunately probably challenge/oppose the grown-up's perception of justice and also their sense of power and control. So grown-ups pull rank, thus increasing the sense of loss and inequality for the person with ADHD.

Even a child without ADHD learns to match the tone and pitch of a parent's voice with their mood and they learn to regulate their reactions accordingly. Most children with ADHD are hypersensitive, and with all that over-activity going on in their heads, they learn to filter. But, they also learn to react. So a certain tone or pitch can make them switch off to a point where they completely ignore you. Or they can react with overpowering rage. This would mean that your voice, when used in a certain way, has become a trigger.

Learn to regulate your own voice. Record yourself saying certain DYNAMITE words like: 'NO!', 'Stop', 'Shut up', and 'Why?'

Some DYNAMITE words:

- Why!
- Stop!
- No!
- Get away from there.
- Shush!

Some DYNAMITE behaviours:

- Sarcasm
- Bossiness
- Dishonesty
- Shouting
- Controlling
- Empty or broken promises

There is no 'one size fits all' strategy to supporting people with ADHD. Individual ADHD presentations are indeed unique. Nevertheless there are practical things that help.

- Set a few clear ground rules and discuss them with the child.

- Using the right language: descriptive, specific, and brief can have a positive impact on reducing the cycle of negativity and conflict associated with children with ADHD.

- An instruction that presents information visually may be more effective.

- If you're shouting, then the child is probably not listening.

- Help the child become aware of the things that distract them.

- Allowing the child to express themselves means avoiding curtailing their free will and reducing the amount of times you use DYNAMITE words.

- Keep a log of behaviours that upset you. You may then be surprised to learn that these do not happen as often as you think.

- Tell the child when they are behaving well rather than just when they are not.

- Stay calm and think about why the child is overreacting? Do they feel inadequate, overwhelmed, criticised, fear failure?

- Advance planning is crucial, for a lot of negative behaviour is due to the anxiety of not knowing what is going to happen, for even though the child with ADHD has done the same thing over and over in the past, they may still not remember how.

- I believe that effort is subjective to individual motivation to achieve emotional wellbeing and satisfaction. Stimulate to motivate.

- Above all, start to see the potential in your child. Children with ADHD have unique talents that require nurturing to develop. Start to think of the deficits (obstructive) as assets (productive).

For people with ADHD, attempting or starting most tasks can become dependent on the level of anxiety that arises from the probability of success or failure. The thought of failure may be accompanied by an amplification of negative feelings: anxiety, frustration, embarrassment and humiliation to mention but a few. So be prepared for procrastination, avoidance and clowning around. Try and understand that it is not laziness, it's fear.

Some Aides-mémoires

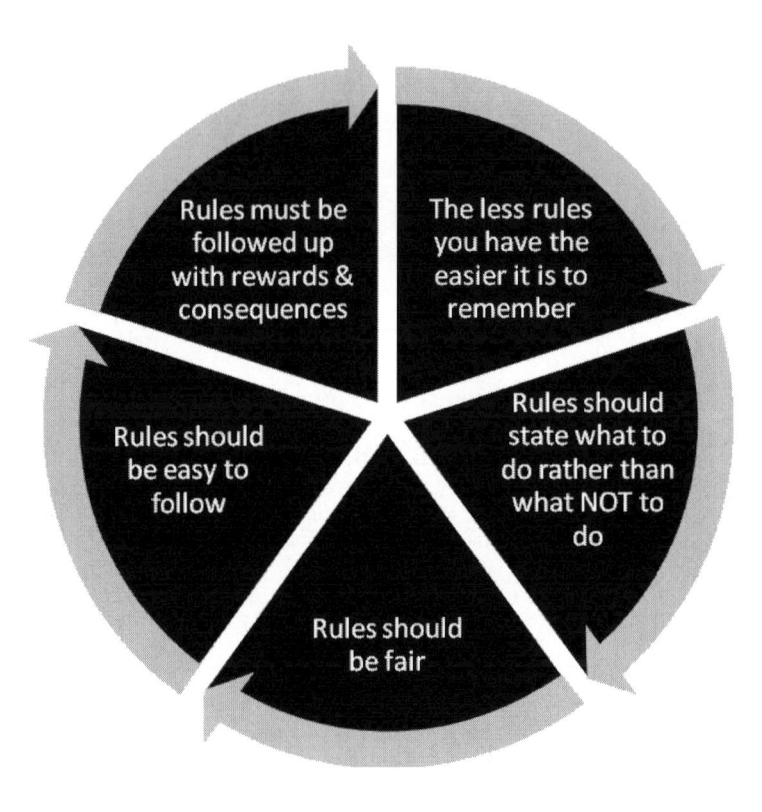

- The less rules you have the easier it is to remember
- Rules should state what to do rather than what NOT to do
- Rules should be fair
- Rules should be easy to follow
- Rules must be followed up with rewards & consequences

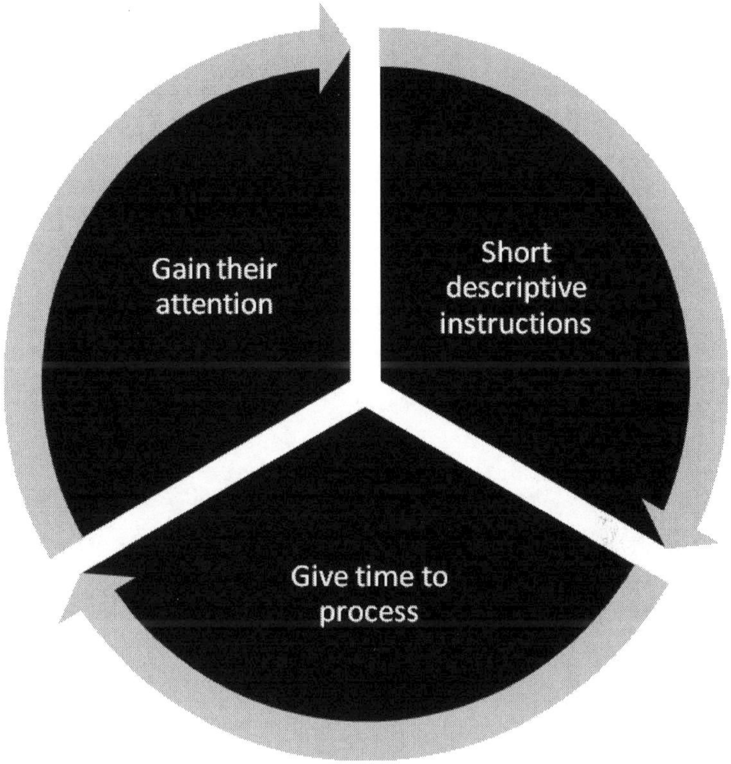
Gain their attention
Short descriptive instructions
Give time to process

Help the child improve the ability to control what they pay attention to.

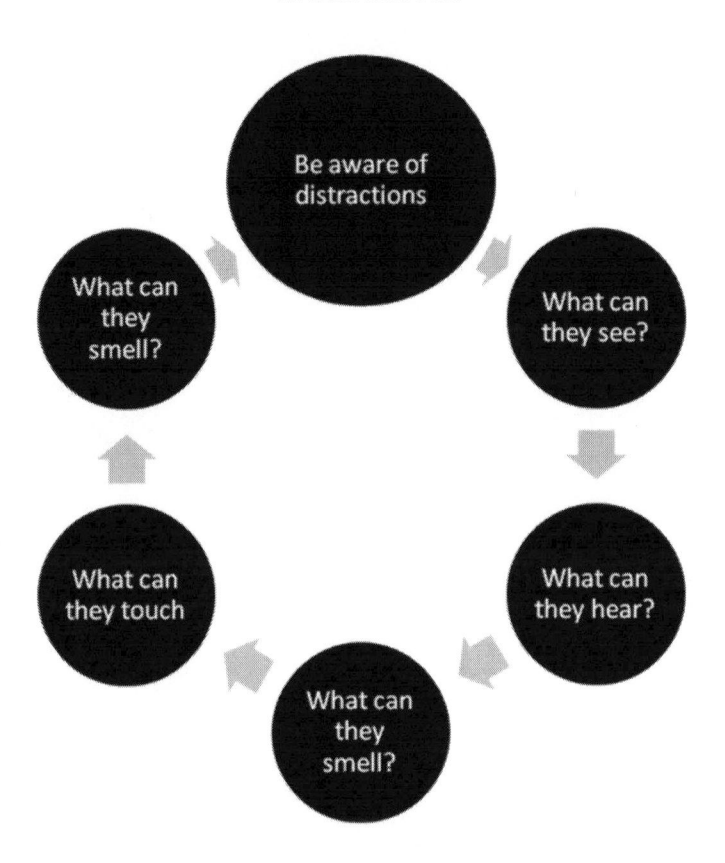

```
        Be aware of
        distractions

What can                    What can
they                        they see?
smell?

What can                    What can
they touch                  they hear?

        What can
        they
        smell?
```

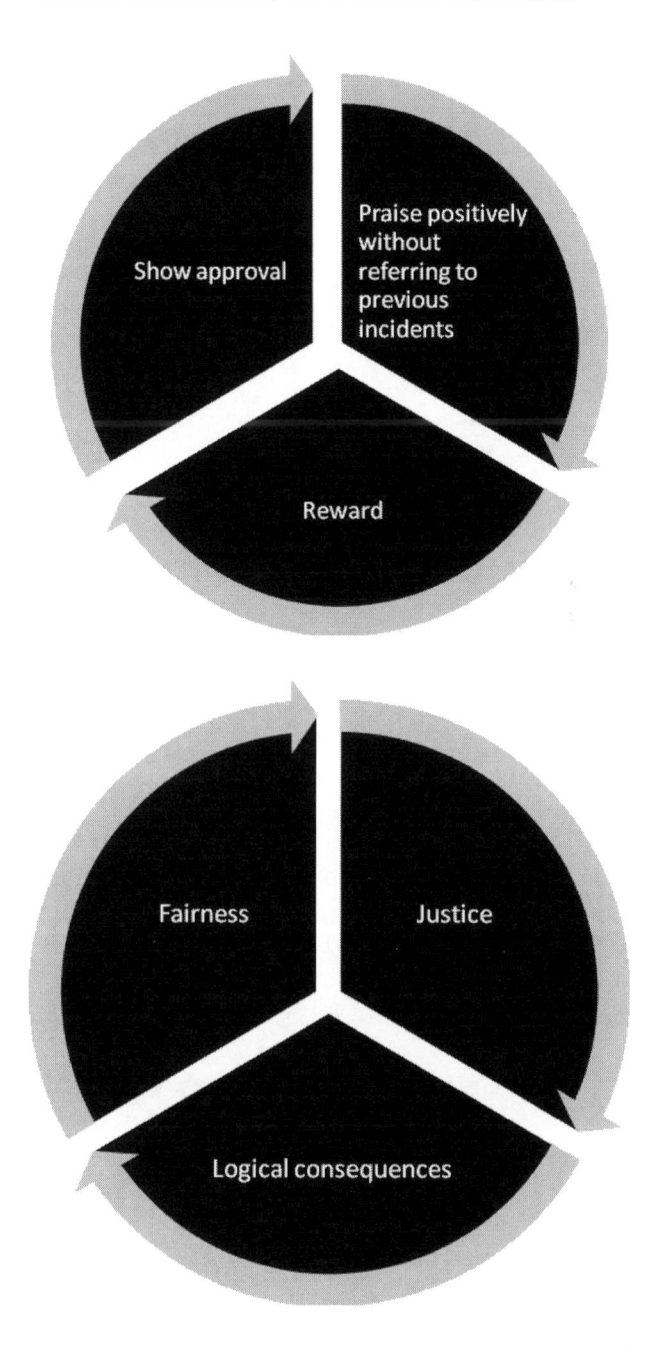

- Show approval
- Praise positively without referring to previous incidents
- Reward

- Fairness
- Justice
- Logical consequences

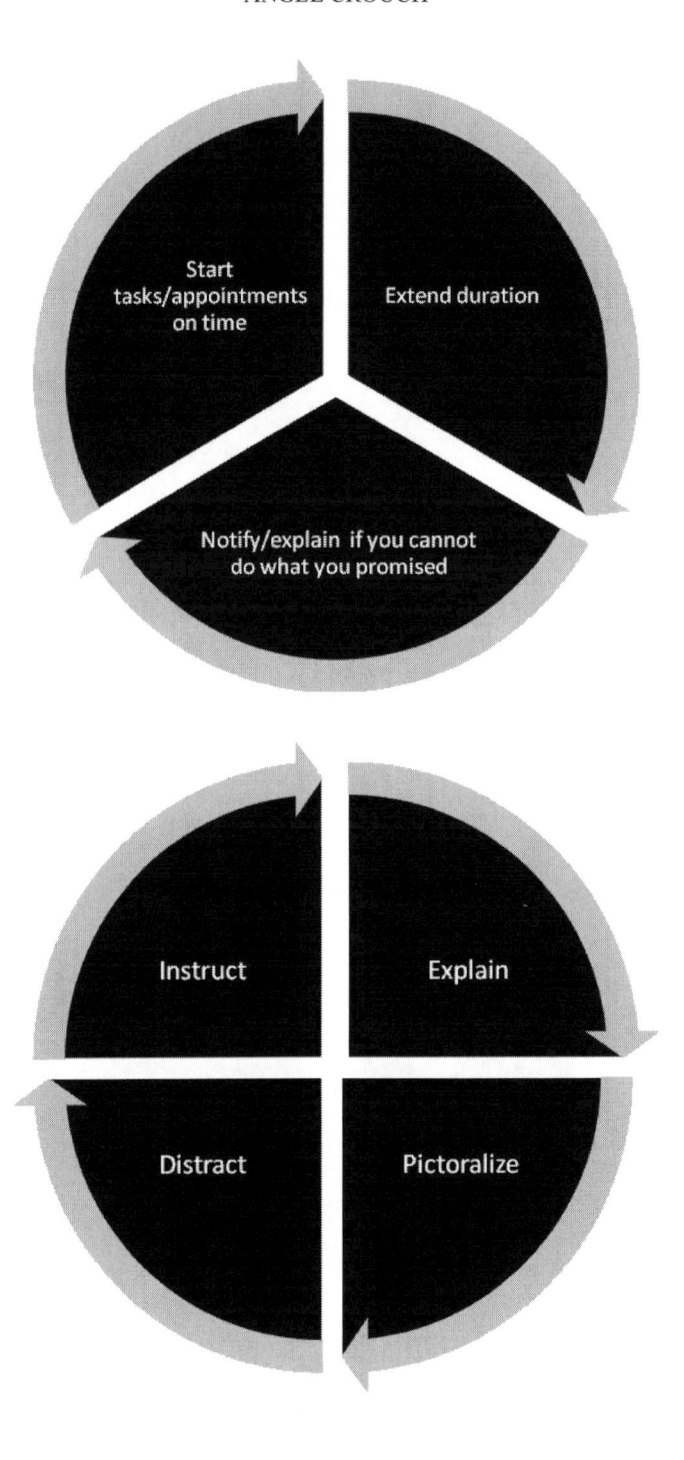

- Start tasks/appointments on time
- Extend duration
- Notify/explain if you cannot do what you promised

- Instruct
- Explain
- Pictoralize
- Distract

SENSORY PROCESSING

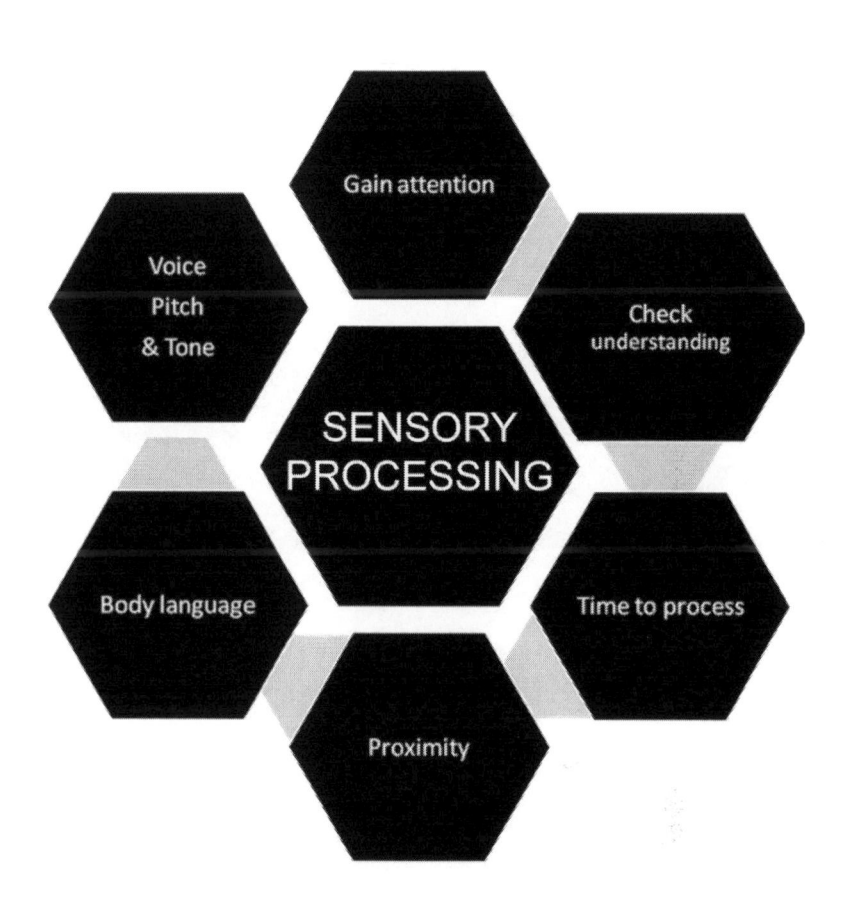

- Gain attention
- Voice Pitch & Tone
- Check understanding
- Body language
- Time to process
- Proximity

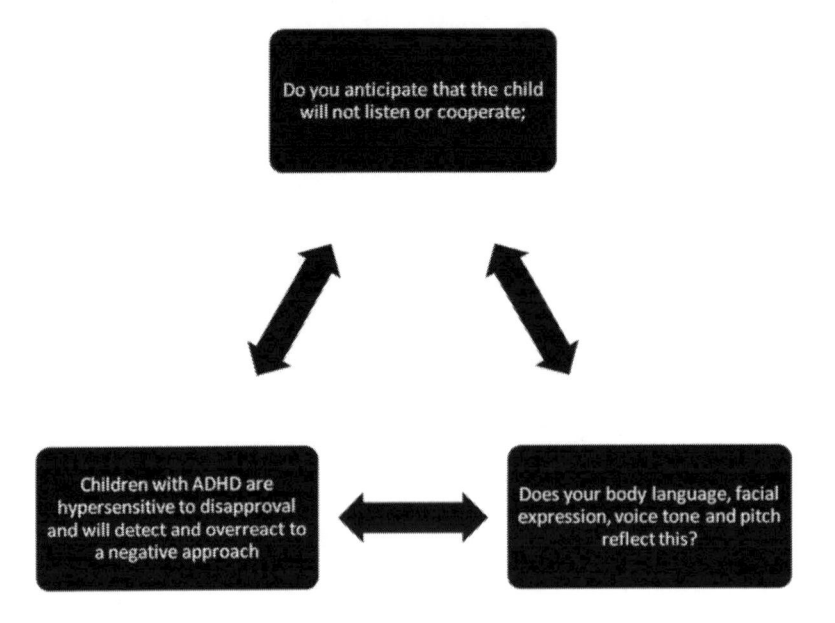

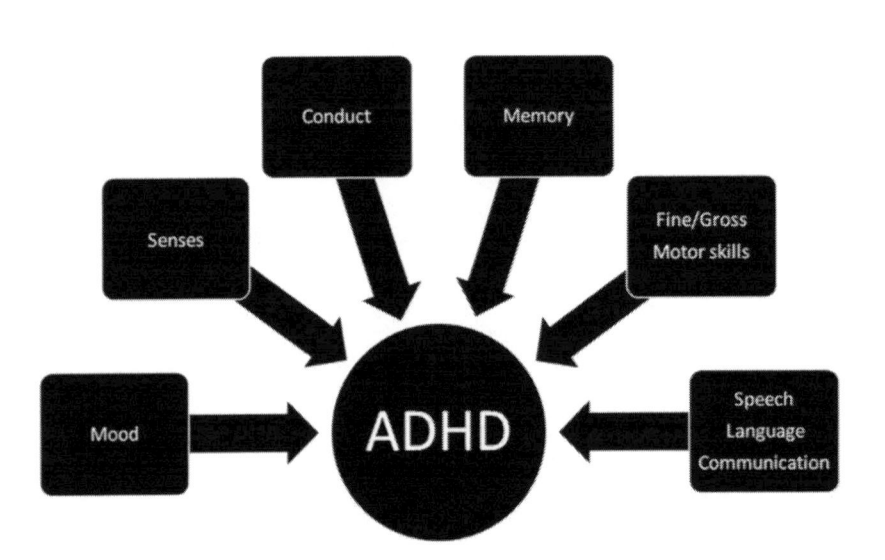

```
┌─────────────────────────────┐
│ Do you anticipate that the  │
│ child will not listen or    │
│ cooperate;                  │
└─────────────────────────────┘
          ↕           ↕
┌──────────────────┐   ┌──────────────────────┐
│ Children with    │   │ Does your body       │
│ ADHD are         │↔  │ language, facial     │
│ hypersensitive   │   │ expression, voice    │
│ to disapproval   │   │ tone and pitch       │
│ and will detect  │   │ reflect this?        │
│ and overreact to │   │                      │
│ a negative       │   │                      │
│ approach         │   │                      │
└──────────────────┘   └──────────────────────┘
```

- Conduct
- Memory
- Senses
- Fine/Gross Motor skills
- Mood → ADHD ← Speech Language Communication

ADHD can influence core functions

The Sound of ADHD (Making Sense of Interference)

When some children with ADHD were asked what it feels like to have ADHD they said the following:

- It feels like a blender
- Everything's so mixed up
- Tumble dryer
- My head is full of noises
- It makes my mind's go blank
- My head feels like it's going to explode
- My thoughts are all mixed up
- Tornado
- "It makes my head hurt!"
- I can't think straight
- It's like my head is a computer and I've got a thousand tabs open

There are too many sensory distractions for a child or young person with ADHD, which is one reason why I think it is so difficult for them to be attentive. They may find one or all sensory distractions – sight, sound, smell, taste and touch – difficult to ignore, and are unable to filter out irrelevant stimuli. The common background sights, sounds and smells that most people take for granted as normal everyday stimulation may well create genuine distractions for the child with ADHD.

As children get older, they may learn strategies to help them to focus, but when they are too young to understand what ADHD is and how it affects them, it's the job of the adults in their lives to help them learn such strategies.

One of the biggest problems facing a child with ADHD is learning how to filter out these different distractions. So how can we help them?

- Try to place yourself in their shoes and learn to listen in a different way.

- Try to listen more actively and become more aware of all the different distractive smells, sights and sounds in your environment. Reducing the number and levels of distraction may make it easier for your child to concentrate.

- For instance, think about when and where you tell your child do their homework.

- Is the clock ticking audibly?

- Does the radiator hum?

- Does the tap drip?

- Does the door hinge creak?

- Is the washing machine or tumble dryer on?

- Is the microwave or electric oven whirring?

- Is someone else tapping away on a computer keyboard?

- Is the TV on in the background?

- Is the lighting casting shadows?

- What does each room smell like?

- Is there a window where people, pets, birds and insects passing by are visible and audible?

- Is the room too silent? There is no such thing as complete silence for people with ADHD. Your child will pick up sounds that you cannot hear. Also, for a child who is used to ongoing activity, silence becomes an unnatural occurrence.

- Noises like the wind or radio waves are ever present and we all hear these sounds differently. I for instance perceive radio waves as a buzzing sound, while someone else with ADHD described it as a humming noise.

- So a lot of these children are hypersensitive to silence.

Believe it or not, soft music (classical or instrumental) playing in the background can help your child concentrate. Try and create as normal an experience for them as possible, which means you have to artificially create distractions when they are absent.

Complete silence may be uncharacteristic for a person with ADHD, so asking them to work in a completely silent space will not work for most.

Chapter 9

Self-reflection

For years I believed that I had ADHD, but I was wrong. I now have diagnosis of Post-Traumatic Stress Disorder (PTSD) and depression. My biggest problems were always anxiety and a fear of failure, and these have had a pervasive effect on my life.

The similarities between ADHD and PTSD mean that both conditions can be difficult to diagnose correctly. It also means that if a child's condition is misdiagnosed, then the primary condition will **not** be treated. Of concern is the fact that of the two conditions, only ADHD can be treated with medication. For children with PTSD who are misdiagnosed with ADHD and treated with medication, the implications really are life changing.

All the symptoms in the graphics next pages are common to both ADHD and PTSD.

ADHD: REFLECTIONS ON A HIDDEN DISABILITY

- Hyperactivity / Fidgety / Restless
- Avoidance / Procrastination
- Impaired Memory
- **LOW SELF-ESTEEM**
- Makes Noises & sounds
- Obsessions / Fixations / Addictions
- Hyperviligance

```
        Depression
Fear of           Irritability
failure           Anger
        ANXIETY
Impulsivity       Sleep
                  problems
        Irrational
        Mood Swings
```

The following excerpts are from my reflective journal and are descriptions of some of my manifestations. They could apply to both ADHD and the range of co-morbid conditions including PTSD.

I hope they help to aid your understanding of a condition that at times can be quite debilitating.

"If I had been able to succeed more in school, I would have developed more positive feelings about myself and maybe have tried harder to succeed in life. Unfortunately I always saw myself as a failure."

"When I talk to other people, I am never sure of how close to stand to them. If a voice is too loud, too, the words ambiguous, or the pitch too loud then I switch off immediately.

If I stand too far away, I may not catch/hear all that is said.

If I stand too close which helps me focus, I may stumble because of your proximity, I may lean in too close, I may lose balance or miscalculate the distance between us and accidentally bump into you."

"One thing that makes me really angry is when I think someone has criticised me. Sometimes they don't even have to say anything. I can see it in the way they look at me. This winds me up something big and my mind starts plotting straight away about how to get them back. Sometimes I can't think about anything else and therefore don't even hear someone else calling me. When I am in this mode the only way to get my attention is not by shouting at me or poking me, but by approaching me from the front. If you shout at me or touch me because I will probably react with aggression without realising it."

"I have odd impulsive recall where a specific memory is triggered, and it can feel like a déjà vu experience but sometimes, the sequence gets mixed up. Alternatively when something happens in real time, I can think it was a previous memory even though it has only just happened. The usual consequence of this is that I get disbelieved and a called liar or deceitful etc."

"I often have trouble filtering or separating different sounds so for instance sometimes when in conversation with someone, I struggle to hear some words clearly and may misinterpret the phonic sounds. Consequently, I often think someone has said something that they really haven't."

"In a loud room or space where there are several conversations taking place, it is really difficult for me to give my attention to the person talking to me as I am distracted by the other voices and the variety of tone and pitch."

"Although it may not seem like it, I do self-reflect on stuff. After an incident and I have had time to calm down, I will suddenly get angry again only this time at myself. I'm angry because I am ashamed that I lost control of my temper again and inadvertently offended someone else yet again."

"My levels of depression can be worsened by my daily experiences of negativity.

Depression also makes my concentration worse and sometimes I can't think straight and remembering things is suddenly more difficult. So making decisions becomes even harder."

"It is sometimes hard for me to see anything good about myself as people often mock me when I make a mistake and can't do something correctly."

"I have difficulty organizing and sequencing detailed information. In addition, my ADHD often makes me process information at a very quick rate yet I don't have the fine-motor coordination needed to 'keep up' with my thoughts. This can make my thinking process confused."

"I can honestly say that my experiences at school were not happy. I experienced anxiety and frustration about prolonged failure on a range of curriculum subjects. This knocked my confidence about learning."

"I have a rigid moral code which means that I stick up for myself when I perceive that I have been treated unfairly. I may not always be right with my perceptions and may get my arguments mixed up or contradict myself but I would ask you to understand that ADHD does affect my ability to reason and empathize."

"My ADHD may affect my oral language functioning so sometimes I may have trouble hearing all of a conversation and/or waiting until the other person has finished speaking, or finding the right words to respond, or I may pause before answering direct questions. I am sure you recognise that this puts me at a social disadvantage especially as language is central to my relationships with others. Just because I appear confident doesn't mean I am."

"My hyperactivity affects me both physically and mentally which means not only do I have trouble settling down but also have trouble switching off."

"I have difficulty expressing thoughts in writing which means I easily get confused and thus have very little motivation to write. Sometimes when trying to

spell a word, I become stuck and my mind can go blank. This is very frustrating for me. So often, because I anticipate that I may fail or not be good at something, I get really anxious which makes me unconsciously avoid it. Unfortunately I think that a lot of my teachers interpreted this avoidance behaviour as laziness."

"Over the years, I believe I may have developed some perfectionistic expectations in order to deal with my anxieties at school. I hate to make a mistake which is why I sometimes destroy my work when I'm displeased with it. Yet having ADHD or PTSD means that I will make many 'careless' mistakes."

"The more I experience consequences for my specific difficulties the less motivated, enthusiastic, optimistic and self-confident I will become."

"If I continue to meet failure and frustration, then my feelings of inferiority are reinforced and I then feel that my effort makes very little difference."

"I get frustrated – because I keep making the same mistakes over and over again; I get anxious when I'm told I have to do something that I know I'm going to fail at and I get angry when I am made to a task which I subsequently fail at, as I knew I would. I get angry at myself for trying and at others for putting me in such a position."

Chapter 10

Some FAQs

Hopefully by now, a lot of the frequently asked questions will have been answered. Nevertheless, here are a few more explanations

Q: Why do children with ADHD make noises and sounds that irritate others? (This could be: Meowing, barking, chirping, beatboxing, and rapping, mimicry, screeching, grunting, humming, flicking [tongue against roof of mouth], screeching, shrieking etc.)

A:

- Sensory issues – oversensitive hearing may cause child to make noises to block out discomforting sensory input and minimise other sources of stimulation by making their own noises.

- Vocal tics – coughing, clearing throat.

- It is not inconceivable to imagine that with all the sensory distortions some activity is identified as voices. These could well be impulsive thoughts or a vivid moment of recall where an event is replayed as if it just occurred.

- Impulsivity – blurting out or copying sounds they can hear.

- Hyperactivity – expressing how they feel.

- A coping mechanism, i.e. when a child experiences an overwhelming negative emotion like anxiety, frustration, shame or embarrassment… making noises or sounds creates a distraction from an uncomfortable persistent feeling or sensation.

- Contentment – like singing in the shower, except singing is replaced with sounds like buzzing, barking, beatboxing, etc.

- Social embarrassment. A sudden recall of an incidence of perceived injury to their self-esteem can trigger an outburst of noises) similar to that suffered by Tourette's sufferers, e.g. inability to stand up for oneself, like being humiliated/bullied, ignored by a member of the opposite sex, or voices.

- Maybe the child can't hear their own voice amidst all the noises in their own head.

- Remember the key here is individual perception.

Q: Why do children with ADHD have such a rigid perception of justice and injustice?

A:

- Problems self-monitoring, evaluating the outcome of thoughts and actions and regulating emotions.

- Causes them to see things in black and white.

- They have a simplistic view of what is right/wrong or good/bad with no sense of consideration for pertaining circumstances.

Q: Why do children with ADHD tend to overreact?

A:

- Emotional hypersensitivity is a trait of ADHD so children with it are more likely to exhibit significant anxiety in social situations, and attack is a defensive coping mechanism.

- The inability to think things through and see it from another person's view is hard to understand.

- Having been criticised, reprimanded, and sanctioned from an early age, failure, fear of failure and criticism can cause a build-up of distress, resentment and anger which boils over.

- They hate to fail and are extremely competitive, needing to win/succeed at any cost.

- Literal thinking for a child with ADHD means believing that whatever people say is true. It's that simple, so if you give an ambiguous message, the child may interpret it differently and believe they are in the right, so overreaction is to be expected.
- Stay calm and think about why the child is overreacting? Do they feel inadequate, overwhelmed, criticised, fear failure?

Q: Does ADHD Cause Accidents?

A: Yes!
- Children with ADHD lack a sense of danger.
- They are unable to curb their impulses.
- More likely to experience injury as pedestrians or cyclists.
- More likely to suffer head, burn and bone injuries or accidental poisoning due to their lack of awareness and/or consideration of risk.

Q: Why do children and YP with ADHD steal?

A:
- To feel in control.
- To prove that they are smarter than others.
- To punish or avenge a perceived wrongdoing.
- An impulsive reaction (lack of self-control, i.e. it caught my attention so I grabbed it without thinking) followed by a rigid stance of denial.

Q: Why do children with ADHD say inappropriate things? This could be jokes, racist, sexist homophobic language, etc.

A:

- Their sense of empathy is impaired.
- Impulsivity makes them blurt out their thoughts without filtering.
- They simply don't understand as it is difficult for them to empathise.
- A need for attention.
- A desire to please, belong, amuse, hurt, humiliate…
- Can they really tell the difference at the time?

Q: Why do children with ADHD tend to be adept at deceit?

A:

- Their impulsive nature may cause them to blurt out a response which may well be untrue, but which they then defend or justify at all costs.
- Low self-esteem can generate boastfulness, so they may admit, deny and brag about something and then can't retract it.
- Lies could be motivated by a need, peer pressure, and rebellion or revenge.
- Lies can be a way to mask forgetfulness or inattention. Children may lie to avoid criticism or sanctions, or to avoid dealing with feelings like guilt, blame and shame over what to them seem like everyday failures.
- Don't make your disbelief obvious by saying something like, "I don't believe you," or "Prove it."
- Say: "I know sometimes you say the first thing that comes into your head so take time to think about whether you want to change your first answer." Don't stand in front of them while they do this.
- When they give you the second answer, ask them (if appropriate) if they can you show you any evidence to support their answer.

Q: How do I know what is real about ADHD?

A:

- There is so much conflicting information but...
- What is real are the children with the disorder. They best know how it affects them.
- Establish a connection with the child. Watch, listen and learn to understand them.
- For questions and advice about ADHD, talk to other parents who are the unaccredited specialists of their children or a qualified health care professional.

Q: Why do children with ADHD have trouble remembering things?

A:

Apart from the obvious deficits in working memory, other things can get in the way:

- Impulsivity.
- Depression, anger, frustration and anxiety can all worsen the memory.
- Sensory overload.
- Sequencing discord.
- Problems with sequencing often lead to distrust! When an incident occurs and an ADHD child is asked what happened, they are rarely able to recall accurately. They may reverse the order of events. They may relate a previous incident, believing it to be the current one. This can particularly cause problems at school.
- The usual reaction to this is disbelief, possibly followed by inferences or accusations of lying. This offends the perception of

justice in the ADHD child as they believe what they are saying is true, so it reinforces their belief of unfairness and persecution.

- One nine-year-old boy was excluded for hitting another pupil. He claimed that the other pupil hit him first. The other pupil denied doing this. Both pupils were telling the truth. The boy with ADHD was hit by the other pupil three days earlier. He did not react at the time. But on this day, three days later, he had a moment of recall where he believed that the pupil had only just hit him and so he hit back.

The problem was, no one believed the boy with ADHD, so he was excluded. He was disbelieved. He was reprimanded and he was made to apologise. Four separate incidences of injustice that will fester and thus embitter him. I have no doubt that the boy with ADHD will get his revenge. Unless someone helps him talk this through and help him resolve it.

Chapter 11

Conclusion

Having ADHD does not mean that the children are stupid or silly or deliberately badly behaved, these children just have different brains. Think about it like being left handed and having to learn to use your right hand. These children just need to be understood and encouraged.

Using the right language (descriptive, specific, and brief) can have a positive impact on reducing the cycle of negativity and conflict associated with children with ADHD.

Decrease social exclusion, increase praise and rewards. Change the way you give instructions. Be aware of your own voice levels. Think about less reactive, retaliatory and punitive consequences.

The transition from childhood to teenager; from teenager to adulthood is sudden and unexpected. For the individual in transition they have to deal with a sudden and unexpected change in attitudes, expectations and treatment. They are suddenly expected to process, self-motivate and organise themselves in response to these changes in attitude.

In the end my message is a simple one. ADHD is a real condition that can adversely affect the lives of subjects and their families. There is no 'one size fits all' strategy to supporting people with ADHD. Individual ADHD presentations are indeed unique.

Think about ADHD more positively and stop using negative labels to describe it. Explain to others that ADHD is not a bad thing. Rather it is a gift. I tell young children with ADHD that they are superheroes with special powers. They just need to be shown or instructed in how to use these gifts.

Some of the ADHD symptoms can be debilitating, while others bestow them with remarkable creative skills and emotional insight. Think Jim Carey, Rory Bremner, Michael Phelps, Solange Knowles,

Justin Timberlake, Michelle Rodriquez. People with ADHD are also: impetuous, instinctive, intuitive, spontaneous, unpredictable, quirky, unconventional, adventurous, daring, outspoken, bold, not easy to hoodwink, adaptable, loyal, creative, enthusiastic, energetic, inquisitive, resilient, risk-takers, caring, good with younger children and older people (who rarely judge them), quick-witted, and intuitive…

Children with ADHD tend to be told or made to feel that the ADHD is a negative, and the cause of all their problems, and that if they didn't have it everyone around them would be happier.

ADHD affects children of every description. Children with ADHD are not possessed by an evil spirit, neither do they practice witchcraft.

One of the most common objections by children with ADHD is that people are always telling them what they can't do, what they shouldn't do, or what they need to stop doing. If people don't tell them exactly what they want them to do, how are they supposed to know?

Consider this: If a child continues to experience frustration and failure then their feelings of inferiority are reinforced, and they feel that their effort makes very little difference. We must start to understand that their differences are normal and instead of trying to change the children:

Whatever you resist will persist.

Change is positive.

Change is necessary.

Change is hard.

The hardest thing to change is the mind – the hardest thing to mind is the change!

Printed in Great Britain
by Amazon